SWEET SUCCESS

A CANDLE BEACH SWEET ROMANCE

NICOLE ELLIS

Cover art by: RL Sathers/SelfPubBookCovers.com

Cover typography by: Mariah Sinclair

Editing by: Free Bird Editing —

Serena Clarke and LaVerne Clark

❀ Created with Vellum

1

"They're sickeningly sweet together." Gretchen Roberts watched as the couple in a booth at the back of Off the Vine snuggled close against each other.

Her friend Maggie punched her lightly in the arm.

"Ouch." She rubbed her arm and glared. "I think you've spent too much time in kickboxing classes."

"Ha ha," Maggie said. "You're happy for her, remember?"

"Okay, okay. I'm happy that Dahlia and Garrett found each other, but I miss spending time with my friend. It's been weeks since the three of us hung out together."

"We've been busy too," Maggie reminded her. "With the mild weather in January and February, this was the biggest winter tourist season we've ever had in Candle Beach." She sipped her glass of Chardonnay and surreptitiously glanced at Dahlia, who was making gooey eyes at Garrett, then rolled her own eyes. "Okay, they're annoying. But I am happy for her. It's been ages since I went out on a date. And what about you? I've got a kid at home, but you're young and single. Why are you sitting here with me on a Friday night?"

"I haven't had time to meet anyone. And I have better things to do with my time than try to meet men." Gretchen grabbed an onion ring from the basket in the middle of the table and crunched down on it.

"Like what?" Maggie gave her a pointed look as she took the last onion ring and dipped it into ranch dressing.

"Like—" Gretchen started to say, but was interrupted by a woman tapping her on the shoulder. A man stood a few feet behind the woman.

"Gretchen? Maggie? I'd heard you were back in town, but what luck running into both of you here." The woman pushed back the artfully arranged curls that hung down her back and gave Gretchen's shoulder a quick squeeze. The scent of floral perfume followed her every movement. Gretchen stared at the woman, unsuccessfully trying to place her.

Maggie recovered first. "Stella, how nice to see you."

Stella beamed at her. "Girls, this is my husband Lance. I'm living on the East Coast now, but we were in Seattle visiting my family and I wanted to show Lance where I spent all my summers growing up. The Washington coast is so different than what we have back east."

They shook Lance's hand and murmured polite greetings. Gretchen leaned back in the booth to get a better look at Stella. Stella's family had summered in Candle Beach and the three of them, occasionally with their friend Dahlia, would spend hours playing together when they were pre-teens. Now, Gretchen hardly recognized Stella as the carefree tomboy she'd grown up with.

"So, Maggie, what are you up to these days? I heard something through the grapevine about a restaurant?" Stella looked around. "Is this it?"

"You heard correctly. But not this restaurant." Maggie smiled at them. "I bought the Bluebonnet Café a few years ago after my son and I came back to Candle Beach."

"And your husband?" Stella asked. "Is he here too?"

Sadness shadowed Maggie's face. "He was killed in Iraq. It's just Alex and me now."

"Oh honey, I'm so sorry." Stella leaned in to embrace her.

"It was a long time ago," Maggie said, with a forced smile. "We're enjoying being back here in Candle Beach and spending time with family. With my husband's Army career, I didn't see much of them for the six years we were married."

"Oh," Stella murmured. "Well, I'm happy you have your family for support." She turned to Gretchen.

"And what about you? What have you been up to?"

"A little of this, a little of that. After college, I moved back here and joined my parents at their company, Candle Beach Real Estate. With the increase in tourism over the last ten years, business has been booming."

"Oh. Well, that's nice for you. I'm sure your parents appreciate your help. I know my parents would love to see Lance and me more often, but with his career on Wall Street and my position at the law firm, we don't get to take much vacation time. I'm up for partner this year." She wore a self-satisfied smile.

"Wow, that's great. Congratulations." Gretchen's stomach flip-flopped. Stella obviously led a successful life and didn't hesitate to boast about it. Her old friend deserved to be proud of herself, so why did Stella's comments bother her so much?

Before she could stop herself, she blurted out, "Actually, I'm in the process of moving to Seattle. I'm branching out from my parents' business and plan to start my own real estate firm there."

Maggie raised an eyebrow, but didn't say anything.

"How exciting," Stella cooed. "Seattle has so much going on. You'll love it." Behind Stella, Lance shifted from foot to foot and looked longingly at an empty booth in the corner of the restaurant. He cleared his throat.

Stella looked at her husband and laughed. "We'd better get going. We've been driving all day and we're starving." She looked around Off the Vine. "This place is so cute. Who'd have thought there would be a wine bar in little old Candle Beach." He tugged at her arm and started to lead her away. She called over her shoulder, "It was nice seeing you, girls." She gave a little wave and allowed him to direct her to the empty booth.

When she was out of earshot, Maggie said, "Now that was a blast from the past. I haven't heard from her in fifteen years."

"Yeah, and we probably won't for another fifteen." Gretchen pushed her dark wavy mass of hair behind her ears and sipped the margarita. Over the top of the glass, she glanced at Stella and her husband, who were engrossed in the menu offerings.

"So what was that about moving to Seattle? Are you really thinking about it? Or were you just saying that because Stella was so full of herself?"

Gretchen shrugged. She'd come up with the idea on the spur-of-the-moment, but now the seed of a plan sprouted in her brain. "I need to figure out what I want to do with the rest of my life. I don't want to be a property manager for Candle Beach Real Estate forever. I love my parents and all, but working for the family business was never something I wanted for my future."

"So this is real? How long have you been considering this?"

"Yes, it's real." She looked toward the window. Outside, the light had faded and the street was empty. "I'm going to move to a bigger city and be a real estate agent. Maybe it won't be Seattle, but somewhere around that area. I want to help people buy and sell their homes and have more of a relationship with clients. I can't do that with the nightly cottage rentals to tourists." As soon as the words left her mouth, she felt a strange sense of relief, as if a weight had been lifted off her chest and she could breathe again.

Maggie put down her wine glass. "So you're really leaving Candle Beach?"

"Yes. I've got to get out of here. This town is suffocating me. The coast is a great place to visit, but it doesn't provide many career opportunities."

"What about being a real estate agent in Candle Beach?" Maggie fiddled with her napkin. "I'd miss having you around. You're one of the few people over the age of five that I hang out with. My parents are always busy and even Alex is so obsessed with his Legos right now that he doesn't have time for me." She smiled, but her eyes were bright with unshed tears.

Gretchen smiled gently at her and patted her hand. "I'd still come visit, and I'd only be a phone call away. Don't worry." Her mood darkened. "But if I stay in Candle Beach, I'll always be competing with my parents for clients. Or worse yet, working for them the rest of my life."

"Starting over somewhere else will be risky. Do you have any money saved for the move?" Maggie asked. "When I bought the café, it took all the money I had left from Brian's life insurance after setting up a college fund for Alex. Even after that, it seemed like every day brought more unexpected expenses. Do you really want to move somewhere without a safety net?"

As always, Maggie was right.

"I don't have much in my savings account." Her optimism deflated. "I guess I could rent out the house Grams left me and lease a smaller place to save money, but I don't really want to do that. I'm not much of a waitress, so working at the Bluebonnet Café wouldn't work, but maybe Dahlia would hire me for a few shifts at To Be Read during the summer tourist season."

"Okay," Maggie said slowly. "So what about clients? You'll be starting over in Seattle. Here, you know everyone. This town isn't all tourists, you know. Locals and new people need houses too."

"I don't know what I'll do about clients." She leaned back against her seat. This was getting more and more complicated, but she knew she couldn't stay in Candle Beach much longer without going crazy. Her face brightened as she thought of something. "Dahlia's mother is a real estate agent. I bet she'd help me make some connections. Maybe her company is hiring."

"Maybe," Maggie said. They looked over to the booth where Dahlia had sat, but she and Garrett were gone. A waitress was clearing away the dishes from the table.

Someone waved at Maggie from across the room. She waved back and nodded at two men. One appeared to be in his sixties, with graying hair and a jovial face. The other was closer to her own age. Both were dressed in the casual uniform of tourists—jeans and polo shirts.

"Who was that?" Gretchen asked. She'd never seen them before.

"Oh, visitors who came into the Bluebonnet Café today. I

took over Belinda's tables while she was on break and they were seated at one of them. Nice guys. I chatted with them for a while about some of the local tourist attractions."

"Oh, you mean like the old well house and the pioneer cemetery?" She waggled her eyebrows mischievously.

"Ha ha," Maggie said. "I mean things like fishing at Bluebonnet Lake, or the whale-watching excursions they can charter down at the marina. There's a lot to do in Candle Beach."

"If you say so." She gulped the watery remains of her margarita and looked at her watch. "I think it's time to head home. I told my parents I'd man the booth at the chocolate festival tomorrow."

"It'll be crazy with all the tourists in town for that. My pastry chef has been working like a madwoman to create new chocolate desserts to showcase." Maggie finished her drink and waved the waitress over for their check.

After the check arrived, they split the bill, waved goodbye and went their separate ways. Gretchen put her hands in her coat pocket and walked up the hill towards the house she'd inherited from her grandmother. She'd felt adrift after college and had moved home while she decided what to do with her life, but the years had passed faster than she'd like to admit. It seemed like yesterday that she'd returned to Candle Beach after graduation, but it had already been ten years. It was time for a change, but how feasible would it be to start over in Seattle? There were so many unknowns, from money and how to earn it, to how easily she'd be able to get clients in a new location. She didn't know many people outside of Candle Beach, so she'd be on her own.

She trudged up the incline and stopped in front of her

house. The lovely Craftsman with the partial water view had been her home since her grandmother died seven years before. She didn't want to rent out the house and move somewhere else, but if that was what it took, it needed to be the top item on her list of money-making ideas. As she contemplated renting out the house, her boxer dog, Reilly, must have heard her footsteps, because he pawed at the front window. She smiled. It was nice to have someone to come home to.

Cheers filled the offices of Gray and Associates as Parker Gray's co-workers raised plastic glasses of champagne to toast his brother, Graham. He raised his own glass in a half-hearted manner and chugged the bubbly liquid. The sweet and sour tang burned on the way down.

A woman put her hand on his arm. "Isn't it great how much business Graham's brought in?" she gushed. "And to be the highest seller for six months straight. What I wouldn't do to be in his place."

Parker gently removed her arm and backed away. "Uh-huh. It's great." He threw his champagne glass in the trash and exited the room. The cube farm where his desk was located was dark and empty with everyone else at the party. He leaned back in his swivel chair and picked up a rubber ball stamped with the Gray and Associates logo from a basket of them by his desk. A yellow sticky note on his computer informed him that Graham wanted him to research a possible new commercial acquisition. Parker hated commercial real estate, but his brother had decided that a Gray needed to be at the helm of the commercial division.

Light streamed out of one of the few enclosed offices in the building, drawing his attention. He stared toward the light. Out of three offices, one belonged to each of his parents and one to his big brother Graham, the golden boy. He tossed the ball in the air and caught it, over and over again. If he stayed at the family's real estate firm, he'd always be overshadowed by his brother. For the umpteenth time, he wished he'd been forward-thinking like his younger siblings and gone into another career field. But the truth was, he loved what he did. He just didn't want to do it at Gray and Associates.

The problem was, Haven Shores wasn't a big city. He wasn't sure if there was room for another real estate company. But he had to try. He didn't want to be stuck in his brother's shadow forever. Things usually came easy for Parker—jobs, women, money—and he wasn't sure why he was letting Graham's success get him down.

"Hey, Parker." A woman in her twenties approached him, her suit jacket barely concealing the not-so-professional low-cut blouse she wore under it.

"Hi, Angie." He threw the ball in the basket.

"Are you busy later? My dinner date canceled and I'd hate to be alone on a Friday night." She pouted her pretty pink lips.

He considered her offer for a moment. If he wanted to create a successful future, he needed to start taking himself seriously. No more women for a while. He had a shot at a big commission and he needed to put everything he had into making it a reality. It was the key to starting out on his own.

"Sorry, Angie." He grabbed his jacket off the back of the chair. "I've got a hot date tonight with some market research."

She pouted again and jutted out her hip. "Are you sure?"

"Yeah, I'm sure. Thanks for the offer." He brushed past her and exited the office. His buddies would never believe he'd turned down a pretty girl, but then again, he'd never been more serious about any undertaking in his life than he was about this opportunity.

*E*arly Saturday morning, Gretchen unlocked the door to Candle Beach Real Estate and retrieved the items she'd need for the chocolate festival. To promote the company, she'd commissioned small chocolates in the shape of a 'For Sale' sign from Chocolate Delights in downtown Candle Beach. She packed the large box of individually wrapped chocolates into her car, along with the canvas show tent and a folding table.

The Marina Park was a mess. She came there often with Reilly, but she hardly recognized it now. People had parked haphazardly on the grass to unload their cargo, blocking others from entering the park. The event organizer was rushing across the grounds, checking off each participant's name on her master list. A majority of businesses in town had volunteered to take part in the weekend event, hoping to brighten what had been a long winter. The Candle Beach Chamber of Commerce had scheduled the event in the slower shoulder season just before the overnight tourist crowd arrived in full force for spring break at the beginning of April.

Off the Vine, along with the other bars and eating establishments in town, had created special mixed drinks that highlighted chocolate ingredients. Local businesses throughout the coastal region offered chocolates and chocolate-based products, including chocolate tea and specialty mochas. The Chamber of Commerce excelled at finding every means possible to separate tourists from their money.

Gretchen spent the morning telling people about all the wonderful overnight lodging options Candle Beach had to offer. At noon, a co-worker came to relieve her from her duties. Instead of heading back to the office right away, she perused the other booths spread out over the Marina Park's lawn. Before she reached Dahlia's To Be Read booth, a man called out to her.

"Gretchen, wait up." A Dennis the Menace look-alike in his early thirties jogged up to her, a camera bobbing on a rope around his neck. He got closer and snapped a picture of her.

"Hey, Adam." She pointed to the camera. "I'd better not end up on the front page of the paper." She scrunched up her face. He took another picture of her and grinned.

"You won't," he said. "Well, maybe you'll be in the paper, but not the front page. I think Chocolate Delights will take that honor." He motioned to the booth to their right that was surrounded by a huge crowd of people jostling for a taste of the free chocolate samples.

"I was headed there myself," she admitted. "I had one of the chocolates they made for Candle Beach Real Estate and it was amazing. I'd never have expected a plain molded chocolate to taste so good."

"I sampled a few of their wares myself when I covered their grand opening last month. Their hot chocolate bar is scheduled to open next week. Maybe you'd like to go with me? I remember how much you enjoyed the hot chocolate my mom would make us when we were kids. I'm sure this will be even better." He looked at her hopefully.

She froze. As much as she'd like to be attracted to Adam, the only thing she felt for him was brotherly love.

"I'm pretty busy with the tourist season starting. But thank you for the offer."

Disappointment crossed his face, but he quickly recovered. Her heart twisted. She'd hate to lose his friendship and she hoped she hadn't hurt his feelings.

"Of course, no worries. Let me know if you change your mind." He turned away from her and pointed up the hill to Main Street. "Make sure you don't miss the Bluebonnet Café's chocolate soufflé. I hear Maggie's pastry chef has outdone herself."

"I will, thanks." She smiled at him. "I'd better go if I want to check out the other booths before I'm due back at the office."

Adam nodded and left. She watched as he snapped photos while he walked. This was another reason she needed to leave Candle Beach. She'd grown up with all the available men in town and they were all like brothers to her.

She swiveled around, intent on hitting up the Chocolate Delights booth before she left the Marina Park. Unfortunately, she turned directly into a man she'd never seen before.

"Whoa," he said, steadying her arms to keep her from falling. He nodded at the Chocolate Delights booth. "I've heard their chocolate is fantastic, but I don't think they're in danger of running out."

"Sorry about that." The skin on her face had warmed and it wasn't from the meager sunlight. "I wasn't paying attention." She looked up at him. At five foot two, she was used to men being quite a bit taller than her, but he must have been over six feet tall. "Are you okay?" She'd smacked into him pretty hard.

"I'm fine." He smiled an easy grin that revealed a dimple embedded in one of the most handsome faces she'd ever seen.

"Do you want to brave the masses with me?" He gestured at the crowd.

"Sure, sounds good. I could use a human shield to get through that." She held out her hand. "I'm Gretchen."

"Parker. Pleased to meet you." He wiggled his eyebrows. "Now that we're acquainted, let's get that chocolate."

She laughed, and they crossed the grass to the Chocolate Delights booth to try their luck at pushing through the crowds.

When they got close enough to the front of the line, Parker was able to reach through the people and snag a couple of the sample plates with three assorted chocolates on each. He handed one to her and motioned to a wooden bench on the other side of the park.

"Let's sit down. I'd hate to drop these."

They sat on the bench and Gretchen bit into one of the chocolates. "Oh my goodness. I thought I'd had good chocolate before, but it was nothing compared to this."

He bobbed his head in agreement and devoured his own plate of treats.

"Okay, nothing is going to top that." She checked her purse for a napkin to wipe the chocolate smear off her thumb. Finding none, she licked it off. He laughed.

"Agreed," he said. "I hear the Bluebonnet Café has some great offerings though. Have you had lunch yet?"

Lunch? She gaped at him like an idiot. Was he inviting

her on a date? A plate of samples was one thing, but this sounded like a date.

"Did you want to grab lunch?" he prompted her.

"Uh, yes. Sure. That sounds great." It was as if someone had taken over her brain and was keeping her from saying anything reasonably intelligent. With any luck, the thief would relinquish control by the time they arrived at the café.

He held his hand out to help her off the bench. She took it and smiled at him. His hand was warm and comforting and she wanted to hold it forever. She realized she was staring at him when he gave her an odd look and eased his hand out of her grip.

What are you doing, Gretch? Some strange guy comes to town and woos you with free chocolate. Now you're as gaga over him as Dahlia is over Garrett. This is ridiculous. Act like someone who's been around a man once in a while, or you're going to scare him.

"Are you ready?" he asked.

"Yes, sorry." She picked up her purse and they walked up the hill, chatting about the other booths they'd visited at the festival.

They had to wait twenty minutes for a table at the Bluebonnet Café, but the time flew by. Gretchen felt as if she'd known Parker forever and the conversation flowed easily.

An elderly woman, who Gretchen recognized as one of the Ladies of Candle Beach club members, had struck up a conversation with Parker, and he'd turned away from her to chat politely with the woman.

Maggie came out to check on the baked goods in the

pastry case and saw them sitting in the waiting area. She cocked her head to the side and gave Gretchen a questioning look. "Who is that?" she mouthed.

Gretchen mouthed back to Maggie, "I'll tell you later." Maggie gave her a thumbs-up from behind the counter. Another old woman came through the door, headed for Parker's companion, and Gretchen groaned. Agnes Barnes. They needed to be seated ASAP. The problem with living in a small town for your whole life was that all the adults you'd grown up with continued to see you as the child you'd once been. She didn't want to deal with an inquisition from Agnes about Parker.

Luckily, the hostess called her name before Agnes reached their bench. Gretchen tapped Parker on the shoulder and pointed at the fast-disappearing hostess, then jetted away from the waiting area before Agnes could approach her. She glanced over her shoulder to make sure Parker was following. He said goodbye to the woman he'd been talking with and followed Gretchen into the dining room.

"What was that about? You ran away like the room was on fire." A bemused expression stretched across his face.

She cringed. He'd noticed her abrupt exit. "Sorry, I didn't want to get pulled into a conversation with that woman's friend. She's kind of the town busybody."

He chuckled. "I totally understand. I've encountered the type before."

When they approached their seats, he moved her chair away from the table and put his hand on the small of her back to guide her toward it.

"Thanks." She'd never had a man do that before. It was a nice gesture.

"My mother would never forgive me if I didn't pull out the chair for a woman I was dining with."

This was sounding more and more like a date. She picked up her menu and hid behind it, pretending to be engrossed in the day's specials.

"You're from Candle Beach, right?" he asked. "What do you recommend?"

"Everything is good, but I'm partial to the Reuben. They pile on so much corned beef that you can barely wrap your mouth around it."

"The Reuben it is." He smiled pleasantly at her and set down the menu.

"Have you been to Candle Beach before?" They didn't get many single male tourists in town. She wondered if he was here solely for the chocolate festival.

"I'm actually from Haven Shores, so not too far from here. I've only been up this way a few times before though. It's a beautiful location. In Haven Shores, the dunes block much of the ocean views, but here it seems like the Pacific is within arm's reach from practically anywhere in town."

"It is beautiful. I've lived here all my life with the exception of the time I spent at college." She sniffed the air and pointed to the dessert a nearby diner was devouring. "Is that what smells so good?" The scent of dark chocolate filled the café.

"Or maybe that?" Parker asked. They watched as a woman bit into a piece of layered chocolate cake. Caramel oozed from between each layer, spilling out onto the plate.

The waitress came to take their orders and they each ordered a Reuben and a glass of iced tea. They opted to split a miniature chocolate soufflé and a piece of the caramel chocolate cake.

"The soufflé will take thirty minutes. Is that okay?" The

waitress's pen hovered over her order pad. Her hair was mussed and she appeared to have been running for most of her shift.

Gretchen looked at Parker. "Do you have time?"

"Sure," he said. "That's fine. I'm not in a hurry."

She nodded to the waitress, who scurried away.

"So what brings you to town? The chocolate festival, or something else?"

"Mainly the festival, but I wanted to check out the town as well."

They continued talking throughout their meal. After eating the chocolate soufflé, she remembered to check her watch. Two o'clock? She'd been so absorbed in conversation with Parker that she'd completely forgotten she had a showing at a quarter past two. Even with her parents owning the property management company, she still had to be professional and show up on time.

"I'm so sorry, but I've got to run. I completely forgot an appointment I have in a few minutes."

She was in the process of gathering her belongings when a woman stopped by the table. They hadn't gotten out of the restaurant fast enough. That darn chocolate soufflé.

"Hi, Agnes," Gretchen said. "We were just leaving."

"Oh, this won't take too much time dear." Agnes beamed at Parker. "And who is this young man?"

"My name is Parker, ma'am." He stretched out his hand and Agnes shook it, scrutinizing him.

"I didn't realize our Gretchen had a male friend. Her grandmother was a dear friend of mine."

Gretchen's face reddened and she pretended to be occupied with finding something in her purse.

"Yes, ma'am. We've known each other since our time fighting pirates together in the Caribbean."

How he managed to keep a straight face after that statement, Gretchen didn't know.

"Pirates?" Agnes's face contorted as she processed the nugget of information.

He nodded very seriously. "Yes, ma'am. But please keep it confidential. I really shouldn't have said anything. It was a top secret mission."

Gretchen stifled a giggle. The look on Agnes's face was worth all the damage control she'd have to do later.

Agnes stared at them and then walked away without another word.

"Sorry about that." Parker grinned like crazy. "I sometimes get carried away."

"No," Gretchen laughed. "It was perfect. I wish I had the nerve to say something like that to her." She checked her watch. "I've really got to go. I can't be late for this."

"No problem, it was great to meet you. Maybe we could get together another time?"

"Definitely." She jotted her phone number down on a paper napkin. "Here's my cell phone number." Then she pulled out cash for her half of the bill and handed it to him.

He pushed it back toward her. "It's on me."

"Are you sure?"

"You can pay next time, okay?" He gave her a smile that made her pulse race.

Next time? There was for sure going to be a next time?

"Well, thanks then. I'll see you later." She turned and hurried out of the restaurant before Maggie could catch her and pepper her with questions. She wasn't usually the type of girl who met strangers and went out with them on the spur-of-the-moment. Her normal MO was to plan everything, with the exception of her abnormal split-second decision to move away from Candle Beach. What was happening to her?

It wasn't until she said goodbye to the new clients she met that afternoon that she realized she hadn't gotten Parker's phone number too. Would he actually call? She hoped he would. Any man who could deal with Agnes and her prying was worth a second date.

3

"*G*retchen!" Maggie burst into the property management office early Monday morning and jogged over to Gretchen's desk in the rear of the building. Gretchen looked up from her computer. Her friend's face was flushed and a bead of sweat dripped off her forehead. Maggie grabbed a tissue to dry her face.

"What's going on?" Gretchen asked. Maggie rarely exuded anything but calm, so this had to be big.

"You'll never guess who was in the Bluebonnet Café today." Her words bubbled out in rapid succession.

"Who?"

"Remember those two guys we saw on Friday at Off the Vine? The ones I'd been chatting with at the café?"

"Yeah, so?" Was Maggie trying to fix her up with one of them?

"They came in the café today again for lunch. I saw them and said hi, and we got to talking again." She practically bounced in place. "Guess who the older man was?"

"Uh, some billionaire? My future husband?"

"No, not your future husband." Maggie scowled at her.

"But a billionaire, maybe. I don't know. Anyways, Martin Egglesby is a real estate developer and he's the one who is developing that piece of property outside of town. Ocean-view Estates, I think it's called."

Why was Maggie so excited about a developer? She normally wasn't big on anything involving change. "And this is exciting, why?"

"Because he's looking for a real estate agent to sell the lots in his development." She flopped into the chair across the desk from Gretchen. "This could be your chance for something new and big. And it's right here in Candle Beach."

Her plan had merit. But Gretchen had limited experience selling real estate. She'd mainly been on the property management side of the family's business. However, she'd earned her real estate license a few years prior and kept up to date on continuing education requirements. Whenever there was an opportunity to manage a property sale, she jumped at the chance.

The clattering of a keyboard from the next cubicle over stopped. She lowered her voice so her co-workers couldn't eavesdrop on the conversation.

"They'll want someone with more experience." She shuffled some papers on her desk. Butterflies gyrated in her stomach as she grew more excited about the possible opportunity, but she didn't want to let Maggie know. Odds were slim that they'd even consider her for the position.

"It doesn't hurt to try for it," Maggie said. "And I may have told him that I know a hotshot real estate agent in the local area."

"Maggie! You didn't." Gretchen's jaw dropped and she stared at her friend. "You should have asked me first."

She shrugged and made a face. "I knew you'd say no, so I

took the initiative for you and gave them your name and contact info."

Gretchen slumped in her chair. Now she had no way of getting out of it. She brightened. Maybe they wouldn't call her.

"This could be it, Gretch. And he told me he has other properties in development all over the Pacific Northwest. He's the real deal."

"All over the Northwest?" Gretchen perked up. "If I succeed at this, he might consider me for another property closer to the city. This could be my in. I was worried about finding clients in a new area, but this would give me a ready-made group of prospective clients."

"Not exactly what I was thinking." Maggie frowned. "If you get the chance to sell the houses in this development, you could parlay that into a real estate career in this area."

"I guess." She could tell Maggie was dismayed by the idea of her leaving and she didn't want to upset her further. "So is he going to contact me, or should I reach out to him?"

"He said he'd call you tomorrow. Isn't this fantastic?"

Gretchen's heart pounded and she didn't answer. She fingered the rough edges of the arm of her desk chair. Maggie's words echoed in her head. Was this fantastic news?

Maggie didn't seem to notice her hesitation. "Speaking of good news, who was that man you were with at the Blue-bonnet Café?"

"Huh?" Gretchen said, still mentally processing the job news.

"The good-looking guy you were with? Super tall? You both had Reubens for lunch. Is this ringing any bells?" Maggie searched Gretchen's face.

"Oh yeah, Parker. I met him at the chocolate festival." Maggie's words registered. "How did you know we both had

Reubens? Were you spying on us?" She looked at her with suspicion.

Maggie grinned impishly. "I was monitoring the situation." She placed her palms on the desk between them. "Tell me everything. I'm living vicariously through you."

"There's not much to tell. We sampled chocolate together and then had lunch at the Bluebonnet afterward. He was a nice guy, but he hasn't called."

"He hasn't called?" Disappointment clouded Maggie's face. "You looked like you were having such a good time. Did you get his phone number? You could call him. This is the twenty-first century, you know."

"Stop spying on me!" Gretchen said, but she smiled at her friend. "I didn't get his number, so the ball is in his court. I hope he calls, but chances are he won't. He's from Haven Shores, so he's probably busy at work right now. Like I should be." Her eyes drilled into Maggie.

Maggie rose from the desk. "Okay, okay, I can take a hint. Hey, Dahlia asked if we wanted to grab pizza on Wednesday night. Are you up for it?"

"Sounds good."

Maggie left and Gretchen stared at her computer without seeing the text on it.

Then the aroma of freshly brewed coffee filled the room. She got up to stretch and grab a cup of coffee. She waved at her co-worker, who smiled and pretended to be extremely busy. The familiar warmth of the mug cut through her apprehension about the future and allowed her to focus.

She had a lot to think about. She'd tried to get Parker out of her mind, but Maggie's observation about how well they'd gotten along reminded her how badly she wanted him to call her back. And now this real estate development thing on top of that. Neither of those were situations she could control. Her main priority still was to plan for a move to Seattle. To do that, she'd need money, so she needed to look into putting her house on the rental market and find a small apartment to rent while she still lived in Candle Beach.

Gretchen had been slammed by a sudden influx of customers the day before, so the next morning, she grabbed the binder of available rental properties from her co-worker's desk. She opened it and flipped through the listings one by one. Most were either bigger than she'd need and too pricey, or they didn't allow dogs. One looked like a possibility. She ran her finger down the page, noting each part of the description. It was a small studio apartment over a building off Main Street. It came with a dedicated parking spot, but not much else. Although it would be close to work, it would be a huge step down from her full house with a view of the ocean.

She shrugged. There wasn't much of a choice. She noted the landlord's phone number. If she rented this property, she could rent out her own house for three times the apartment's rent and earn money towards her 'get out of Candle Beach' fund.

She dialed the landlord. *Ring, ring, ring.* After a moment of silence, it went to voicemail and she left a message. On to the next item on her list—finding a second job. She didn't have any clients until later in the day, so she picked her purse up off the ground and set off for To Be Read.

When she reached the bookstore, she was pleased to see that it was busy. The foot traffic boded well for Dahlia needing extra help and it made her happy to see that the business was a success. Dahlia was ringing up a customer when she arrived, so she browsed the mystery section while she waited for her friend to be free.

A few minutes later, Dahlia tapped her on the shoulder and she spun around.

"I see business is good," Gretchen said. "Rumor is you make one of the best lattes in town." After a fire destroyed the interior of To Be Read the previous summer, Dahlia had converted a whole corner of the bookstore into a reading nook with an espresso bar. The scent of ground coffee beans filled the air and every seat on the couch and loveseat was occupied. Another group of customers came through the door and milled around the table offering books by local authors that Dahlia had arranged near the entrance.

"Yes, it's been great. I've even had people come up here from Haven Shores. Apparently there are a lot of people who don't like the cold and sterile atmosphere of the Book Warehouse. People have really taken to the new layout of To Be Read." Dahlia looked around the room proudly. "Who would have thought a fire would be the best thing to happen to the bookstore? With the insurance payout, I was able to completely remodel the interior."

"Hey," Gretchen said. "I was wondering...do you need any more part-time employees?"

"Why? Are you interested?" Dahlia straightened a section of books on a shelf while she waited for Gretchen's response.

"Yes, I'm trying to pick up some more hours to add to my savings." She wasn't sure why she didn't tell her friend about her goal to move to the city, but it didn't seem like the right time. For all she knew, Maggie had already spilled the beans to Dahlia.

"I just hired someone to take on a few shifts during the

busy season, but I'll keep you in mind if it doesn't work out or if I need more help." Dahlia looked at her. "You know I couldn't have made this business a success without all the help you and Maggie gave me. I truly appreciate it and I know Aunt Ruth would be proud of how her bookstore has evolved."

"No problem. You're family now. We'd do anything for you." Gretchen gave her a quick hug. "Do you happen to know of anywhere else that might have an opening for part-time work?"

"Did you try Candle Beach Kids? I heard Abby was looking for someone for a few days a week."

"I haven't, but that sounds like a good option. I love that store. I'll try there next. Thanks for the idea."

Gretchen's phone vibrated in her pocket and she took it out to check it. She didn't recognize the phone number. Was it the apartment landlord calling her back? Or could it be Parker?

"I've got to take this," she said to Dahlia. "See you tomorrow night."

Gretchen pushed the 'call' button on her phone and stepped out of the bookstore. A breeze scented with seawater ruffled the spring flowers Dahlia had planted in the window box. With her free hand, Gretchen pulled the edges of her jacket closed to ward off the chill.

"Hello?" she answered.

"Hello, is this Gretchen Roberts?" a man's deep voice asked.

"Yes, this is Gretchen." Static filled the line. The wind was messing with the already precarious cell phone service in Candle Beach. Yet another thing she wouldn't miss about small-town life.

"This is Mareby," said the garbled voice.

Gretchen pressed the phone harder against her ear. She still had no idea who was on the other end. "I'm sorry, I didn't catch that," she said politely. "Are you calling about the apartment?"

The static cleared. "No." The man hesitated. "This is Martin Egglesby. Your friend Maggie at the café told me you were a real estate agent. I'm the developer of Oceanview Estates, a few miles south of Candle Beach on Highway 101."

"Ah, yes. I'm happy to hear from you. Maggie did mention you'd call."

"I'm interviewing potential candidates for selling the new homes in the development." He paused and cleared his throat. "Is this something you'd be interested in?"

Panic froze her for a moment. Was she interested? This could be the best thing to ever happen to her, or it could be the biggest opportunity for failure in her life. Well, she'd promised herself she'd do whatever it took to reach her goals.

"Ms. Roberts? Are you still there?"

"Sorry, the connection was bad for a moment. I'd love to be considered for the position."

"Glad to hear that," he said. "I have an opening on Friday, say about ten o'clock? Would that work for you?"

"Ten is fine."

"Our sales office is located in a trailer at the entrance to the development. Are you familiar with the location?"

Gretchen assured him she knew where it was and they said their goodbyes.

Fear mixed with excitement and her fingers shook so badly that she worried she'd drop the phone. While she contemplated her future interview, the phone vibrated again. Another phone number she didn't recognize showed up on the caller ID.

"Hello?" A thrill shot through her. Was Parker finally calling her? *I wish I'd gotten his phone number,* she thought for the hundredth time. Playing the waiting game was not something she enjoyed.

An elderly man spoke. Her elation disappeared. It wasn't Parker.

"Ms. Roberts?" the man croaked.

"This is she."

"I'm Darrell, the owner of the apartment you called about."

"Oh yes, of course. Thank you for calling me back." Maybe this was her lucky day. Phone calls about a job interview and a new apartment all in the same day.

"I'm sorry to have to tell you this, but I just rented the place out. With all the summer folks, rentals are going fast. I may have something in a few months, but everything I have now is fully rented."

"Oh," she said in a small voice. "Thanks for letting me know." She hung up the phone and sat down on a nearby bench. Dejected, she slumped against the back of the bench. Even the colorful purple and yellow tulips growing in a planter next to the bench failed to cheer her up.

What was she going to do now? There hadn't been any other good options for apartments in the real estate office's rental listings.

After allowing herself a few minutes to feel sorry for herself, she got up and walked down the hill toward Candle Beach Kids. A cheery turquoise sign welcomed her into the brick building. Inside, the vanilla-scented air and natural lighting created an inviting shopping atmosphere.

"Hi, Gretchen. It's been a while. What can I help you with?" the shop's proprietor Abby Lewis asked. She'd wound her dark, curly hair up in a bun, but several tendrils had escaped. She wore a casual uniform of jeans and a turquoise and white t-shirt imprinted with the Candle Beach Kids logo. Gretchen immediately felt at ease. If she had to get a part-time job, this would be a comfortable and fun place to work.

"Hi, Abby." Gretchen picked up a child's t-shirt depicting a crab and emblazoned with the words *I'm never crabby in Candle Beach*.

"Cute." She carefully folded and replaced the garment on the stack of t-shirts. "I need to get one of these for my niece next time she's here visiting."

"It's one of our bestsellers." Abby leaned against the counter. "Is there something in particular that you're looking for?"

"Actually, Dahlia at the bookstore mentioned you might have an opening for part-time help."

"I do," Abby said. "I'm looking for someone to work evenings during the week. Do you know someone who might be a good fit?"

"Me." Gretchen smiled at her. "I'm hoping to pick up some extra hours this summer and I'd love to work here."

"Well, I'd love to have you here too. Can you fill out this employment application by tomorrow? We can talk more about the job after I review your application."

"Sure, thanks. I'll get it back to you tomorrow." Gretchen took the application from Abby and looked it over.

The bell over the door rang and Abby said, "Got to go. Make sure you bring it back tomorrow. I need to make a hiring decision within the next few days." She left Gretchen and crossed the store to greet the customer who had entered.

Gretchen perused the other store offerings then left. The weather had turned chilly and clouds had formed over the ocean in the formerly blue sky. She'd better get home before the weather worsened. March weather was always a guessing game. You never knew whether you'd get gorgeous clear days, or the storm of the century. Sometimes, you'd even get both in one day.

Maybe it was the same with life. In one day, she'd been given a huge opportunity and disappointing news about the apartment. One good piece of news, one bad. She brightened. Maybe Parker would call and tip the scale toward the positive.

For now, she needed to figure out how to earn money immediately. If she didn't get the position at the new housing development, the Candle Beach Kids job would help, but she'd still need more money. Somehow, she'd figure out how to earn the funds to move to Seattle.

4

———

*G*retchen stood in front of her own house and stared at it. When Grams passed away, she'd left it to Gretchen, who'd helped care for her in her final years. The gift of the house had allowed her to move out of her parent's place after she'd returned to the nest following college graduation. Now, it may be the key to moving away from Candle Beach.

The robin's egg colored Craftsman with white trim stood tall on the hillside, surrounded by greenery and colorful flowers. She'd lovingly kept up the gardens that her grandmother had treasured. New buds formed on the trees and bushes, and red and blue tulips peeked out from behind the rocks bordering the edges of the garden beds. Birds chirped and flew in and out of the feeder she'd stocked with seed that morning.

Would tenants treat the house as well as she had? From what she'd observed at the property management company, people rarely took good care of things they didn't own. At least for the time being, she'd be in town to keep an eye on things.

If she wanted to get the house on the market soon, she needed to assess if it needed any maintenance. She pushed the garden gate open and walked along the path to the backyard. A light breeze carried the intoxicating scent of freshly blossomed flowers across the garden. She reached the backyard and pivoted slowly. Other than a few weeds to pull, everything looked to be in good condition.

The carriage house style garage with mother-in-law apartment, accessible from the alley, caught her eye. She'd stored a few things up there when she'd moved into Gram's house. Other than that, she hadn't really thought about it. She'd planned to use the garage as part of the rental listing, but now another idea germinated in her brain.

What if she rented out the main house and lived in the mother-in-law apartment? The apartment over the garage was old and run-down as no one had lived there in over fifteen years, but she didn't need much. She ran up the stairs of the carriage house and unlocked the door.

She ran her finger over the two-burner stove, creating a flock of dust bunnies that flitted in the sunlit air. She plugged the small, rusty refrigerator into the wall. It came on with a thump and then settled into a pleasant hum. The appliances seemed serviceable and would be fine for a few months. She opened the bathroom door in the corner and flipped on the light. Mineral rings had formed in the toilet and a spider scurried across the shower stall. Nothing that couldn't be fixed with a good cleaning.

She'd lose a little money off the potential asking price if she didn't rent the garage too, but the loss would be much less than the cost of an apartment in town. If she rented out the big house, she could earn a sizable amount each month and not have to pay rent to someone else. It was a win–win.

Satisfied with her decision, she skipped down the

carriage house steps and into the big house. She'd list it for rent online and with her office. With any luck, the three-bedroom, two-bath house would rent quickly. She didn't know how long it would take to earn enough to move to Seattle, but she hoped it would be before winter.

The house attracted more potential renters than Gretchen would have anticipated, although based on her own experience with the rental market, she should have known. She had listed it on Tuesday afternoon with her own company and on an Internet rental site. By Wednesday morning, she'd already received three phone calls about the property. One of the callers had been particularly excited about the rental and Gretchen had agreed to show it to her that evening before she met Dahlia and Maggie for pizza.

Gretchen was off work on Wednesday, so she spent a few hours in the afternoon deep cleaning the house and reducing clutter. Although she generally kept a neat and tidy house, there were a few spots that needed work, and with a dog, there was always pet hair to vacuum. At five o'clock, when the prospective renter was due to arrive, the house gleamed and smelled like lemon cleaning solution.

Someone rapped on the door and she shoved the vacuum into the hall closet. She quickly wound her hair up in a messy bun and opened the door. A woman in her late twenties stood on the porch, looking at the porch swing and the gardens. A man leaned against the far side of her car, with his back turned to the house.

"Hi." The woman grinned at her. "I'm Charlotte. You must be Gretchen." She stretched her hand out to greet Gretchen. Her smile was contagious. There was something enchanting about her. She was a petite blonde with wavy hair that reached halfway down her back and she wore a flowered sundress with a navy blue sweater, perfect for spring.

"Yes, I'm Gretchen. Come in and I'll show you the place." She peered at the man outside. He hadn't moved away from his car door. "Is he coming in?"

"Yes, he's just finishing up a phone call. We can get started without him."

"Alright. Well, as you can see, this is the yard and the front porch." She gestured to the space. "As I noted in the ad, I'm renting it fully furnished. I'll continue to maintain the gardens and the lawn. I'll be living in the carriage house, behind the main house, so the backyard will be shared. Does that work for you?"

"Sounds good," Charlotte said. "The yard is beautiful but I'm happy to not be fully responsible for it. The view is amazing." She stared out at the ocean, which was partially visible behind a grove of trees. The sunlight glinted off of her sparkly beaded earrings.

They entered the first floor of the house and Gretchen showed her around. "Here's one of the three bedrooms, the dining room, and the kitchen."

"Oh, I love how quaint the kitchen is," Charlotte said. Gretchen wasn't sure whether to take that as a compliment or not, but she appeared sincere.

They passed by the window to the backyard and Gretchen pointed out the carriage house and the alley. "You can park in the back alley if you'd like. I'll be parking there as well, but you'll have one space by the carriage house. You can also park in front of the house on the street."

Charlotte opened the door and peeked out at the backyard.

"Uh, is your husband coming in?" Gretchen said to the back of her head.

Charlotte closed the door. "Sorry, I couldn't hear you, what did you ask?"

"The man you're with, is he coming in?" She looked back toward the front door. "Should we wait for him before I show you the rest of the house?"

"No, we're fine." Charlotte opened up a closet and nodded approvingly. "There's a surprising amount of storage space in this house."

"The closets upstairs are roomy too. Let me show you the two bedrooms upstairs."

They walked up the stairs and she pointed out the bathroom and the bedrooms.

Charlotte ran over to the street-facing window and looked outside. "I love this. You must spend so much time just staring out at the ocean."

"Not as much as I probably should," Gretchen admitted. "You live here long enough and you start to take things for granted."

"I don't think I ever could. My family is from Haven Shores, but we live closer to the center of town than to the ocean."

Gretchen shrugged and gazed out the window at the expansive ocean. A ship drifted across the horizon on its way to the next port. At this time of the evening, the sun resembled a giant fireball sinking into the water.

"It's getting dark," Charlotte remarked. She turned to Gretchen. "I love the house. Do you have a rental application I can fill out?"

"I have the paperwork downstairs in the kitchen." They returned to the kitchen and Charlotte sat down at the table to fill out the rental application.

Someone knocked at the door. Was it the mysterious husband? How was he not interested in the house he'd be living in?

Gretchen flung open the door and greeted the man, who had his back turned to her. He turned around and her mouth gaped open.

"Parker?"

"Gretchen," he said with surprise. "It's nice to see you. I'm sorry I haven't had a chance to call you."

She could see why he hadn't called. Parker was married? To Charlotte? She couldn't even hate Charlotte because she was so nice. But Parker? She could hate him plenty. What kind of married man took another woman out on a date? A cad, that was for sure.

"Nice to see you," She managed to say through her shock. "I wasn't expecting to see you here."

"Well, Charlotte wanted to see the house, but I didn't know you were the landlord. What a coincidence." He looked around. "It's a beautiful house and piece of property."

"Feel free to look around. Charlotte is in the kitchen," she said. "I need to get something out of my car, but I'll be back in a few minutes."

"Gretchen..." he said.

The blood in her ears roared, making her deaf to his words. She didn't know whether to cry or scream at him. The best plan was to not make eye contact with him.

She led him into the kitchen. Without turning around to face him again, she exited out the back door towards the carriage house and her car. Once safely outside, she took a deep breath. It wasn't like she was highly invested in a relationship with Parker, but she'd thought they had something special.

Sheesh, what kind of bad luck did she have? She looked back toward the house. He stood like a statue at the window, staring at her. She averted her eyes and walked to the car. Reilly barked when he heard her approach the carriage house. She ducked her head inside to shush him.

Outside, she rummaged around in the car and contemplated her options. She could accept Charlotte and Parker's application and then lease the house to someone else. After all, she had several other prospective tenants who wanted to see the property the next day. That seemed a much better choice than to have to see the couple every day and run the chance of running into him in their shared backyard.

But, as a real estate professional, she couldn't in good conscience turn them down simply because she thought Parker was a cheating jerk. That wasn't a legal reason to refuse housing to someone—although it should have been. She'd have to accept the application and evaluate it fairly along with those of the other applicants.

She slammed the car door with a resounding bang and returned to the house.

"So, did you decide to apply for the house?" she asked the couple. To her ears, her voice was bright but hollow. She did her best to avoid looking at Parker.

"Here's the completed application." Charlotte handed her the form, which she'd filled out in bubbly blue handwriting. "Thanks so much. When do you think you'll make a decision?"

"I'll notify you tomorrow afternoon. I'm showing the house to two other applicants tomorrow morning. I'll need some time to run the credit checks and make a decision." She guided them toward the door. "Thank you for your application."

Parker gave her an odd look and then walked down the steps toward the car.

Charlotte looked longingly at the house and then waved at her. "Talk to you tomorrow," she said. "Thanks again."

Gretchen watched them get in the car and drive away. The sky was darkening. She looked at her watch. Almost six o'clock! They had stayed longer than she'd expected. She'd promised her friends that she'd meet them at Pete's Pizzeria for dinner at six. She ran back into the house, applied some lipstick, grabbed her coat, and set out to meet her friends. For once, she had a good story to share with them. They'd never believe it. Her stomach twisted. She wouldn't have guessed Parker would turn out to be a liar like all the rest of the men she'd dated.

5

"You're kidding me." Dahlia set her glass of wine on the table and stared at Gretchen. "So this guy was married? Seriously?"

"I know." She sighed. "It's like I'm a magnet for lying jerks. You never met him, but the last guy I dated wouldn't win any prizes for boyfriend of the year either."

Maggie nodded. "Sorry Gretch, but I've got to agree. Chuck was a jerk. I still can't believe he cheated on you with someone he met at the gas station." She sipped her beer daintily. "I thought this guy had potential though. He seemed really into you."

"I guess appearances are deceiving," Gretchen said. A waitress wound her way across the room and set a Pete's Deluxe pizza down in front of them.

"Let me know if you girls need anything else," the waitress said.

"Thanks, Reba," replied Maggie. She eyed the pizza hungrily. "Yum." She pulled a piece of pizza off the pie and slid it onto her plate. Gooey mozzarella cheese trailed from the pizza tin all the way to her plate.

"Oh my gosh," Gretchen said. The aroma of the pepperoni and Italian herbs mixed deliciously in the air and her stomach rumbled. "This looks fantastic. I didn't realize how hungry I was." She thought she'd lost her appetite after seeing Parker with Charlotte, but it had returned full force. She wanted to tell her friends about the call from Martin, but she didn't want to monopolize the conversation. It could wait until later.

"So what about you two?" Gretchen asked. "How is everything going? Any news?"

Dahlia's eyes danced. "Actually, I do have some news." She pulled her left hand out from underneath the table and held it out to them.

Maggie and Gretchen squealed when they saw the princess cut diamond on her finger.

"He proposed?" Maggie grabbed her hand to get a better view of the ring.

"When did this happen? How long have you been keeping this a secret from us?" Gretchen's mouth twitched as a smile threatened to break through her mock glare.

"Relax! It just happened last night," Dahlia said. "I didn't even tell my parents until this morning."

"How did he propose?" Maggie asked, releasing Dahlia's hand. "We want all the details."

"He took me to dinner at Lilian's in Haven Shores to celebrate the anniversary of the first time we met. He gave me a bouquet of red roses and had arranged for us to have the best seat in the restaurant, with a view of the ocean. I thought that was romantic in itself, and then halfway through the meal, he got down on one knee and proposed." She beamed at the memory.

"I want to see the ring now," Gretchen said.

Dahlia shoved her hand across the table to let her get a closer look at the ring. "It's beautiful, right?"

"Gorgeous," Gretchen agreed, holding Dahlia's hand. The white gold shone as she twisted the ring to examine it.

She wanted to be happy for her friend—correction, *was* happy for her friend—but a little part of her was jealous. She tried to push the thought away. One of her best friends was getting married and was obviously in love.

"Of course, you guys are going to be my bridesmaids," Dahlia said.

They grinned.

"Yay! I'm so excited for you," Maggie said. "With the exception of Alex's birth, my wedding day was the best day of my life."

"When's the wedding?" Gretchen bit into her pizza and looked at Dahlia.

"We're thinking about having it in early December. I want to be able to take a honeymoon, and that wouldn't be possible if we get married in summer. The bookstore is way too busy to take time off during prime tourist season." Dahlia rotated her hand and admired the way her ring sparkled in the overhead light. "Candle Beach will be decorated for the holidays and maybe we'll even have snow. I'd love to have snow in our wedding pictures. I'm thinking red or violet dresses for the bridesmaids?"

Maggie nodded in approval. "You'll have gorgeous pictures, especially if there's snow."

"It sounds beautiful," Gretchen said.

"You'll be a perfect bride." Maggie reached for another slice of pizza.

"I thought about not having a big wedding celebration since this is my second marriage, but Garrett insisted. He's a romantic at heart and wanted a big wedding." Dahlia shrugged. "I'm excited too. I know Garrett's the one I want to spend the rest of my life with, so why not have a formal wedding?"

Gretchen's heart panged. With her luck with men, would she ever experience the happiness that was written all over Dahlia's face? Not that she'd had plans to marry Parker, but how could she have been so wrong about him? They'd seemed to have a very real connection, but she'd obviously missed some major red flags.

The waitress came by to deliver their check. It was now or never to share her good news.

"I had something else..." she began, but was interrupted by Maggie's phone ringing. She stopped talking to allow Maggie to answer it. Maggie chatted with the other person for a minute and her tone became concerned.

Maggie hung up and dropped some money on the table.

"I've got to go get Alex from my mom's house. She said he's running a slight fever. Probably something he caught at school."

"Oh, I hope he's okay," Dahlia said. "I heard there's a stomach bug going around."

Maggie made a face. "I hope it's only a twenty-four hour thing. Last time he had a stomach thing it lasted for five days. Poor kid. Ugh. I'm not looking forward to tonight."

"If you need me to bring you guys soup or orange juice or anything, let me know," Gretchen volunteered.

"Thanks girls, I appreciate it. I'm sorry I have to jet. I always love getting out of the house and spending time with adults." She leaned in to hug Dahlia. "I'm so happy for you and Garrett." She waved goodbye and left.

Well, at least she could share her good news with Dahlia. Gretchen turned to her, but Dahlia had pulled her wallet out of her giant purse.

She fished around in her wallet for some cash and paid her share of the bill. "I've got to run too. I promised Garrett I'd go with him to tell his mom tonight about our engagement." Her face flushed with joy. "I'll see you next week at dinner?"

Gretchen nodded and Dahlia left her alone at the table. She nursed her drink and stared at the last piece of pizza. *Oh well,* she thought. *Might as well eat it.* She wished she'd had a chance to tell her friends about the real estate developer's phone call. It would have to wait until she saw them next. She finished her food, paid the bill, and left.

Gretchen sat at her desk in the Candle Beach Real Estate office and stared at the rental applications for her house. She'd run credit checks on the two parties she'd shown the house to that morning and the news wasn't great. There was no way they'd beat Charlotte and Parker's application based on credit history alone.

Oh well, she could hope some other red flag popped up in their credit check. She sighed and pulled the couple's application out of her file folder. She scanned the information Charlotte had filled out. Parker's information wasn't on the form.

She called the listed number. "Hi, Charlotte?" She tapped the desk with her pen.

"Yes, this is she." A car honked in the background on Charlotte's end of the call.

"This is Gretchen, the owner of the house you looked at yesterday."

"Oh yes, did you make a decision yet?" Her eagerness

came over the phone line. "I'm really interested in your house as I'd like to move to Candle Beach soon."

"Not yet. I had a question about your application." Ugh, she really wished she didn't have to go through all this. She'd rather forget Parker existed.

"Sure, what about?"

"Well, I don't see your husband's information listed on the application. I need all prospective tenants to provide their information so I can fairly assess the applicants."

"My husband?" Charlotte said. "I don't have a husband."

What was she talking about? She didn't have a husband? Gretchen's mind spun. "Parker. Isn't he your husband?"

Charlotte snorted. "Oh, no. Parker's my brother. He came along with me for moral support, not that he was very helpful while we were there. He lives in a condo in Haven Shores and doesn't have any plans to move. It's just me."

"Oh." Gretchen was quiet for a moment. She'd been awfully cold to Parker when he was at her house because she'd misunderstood the situation. "Uh, I'll run your information and let you know about the house within the hour. Sound good?"

"Sure, thank you," Charlotte said brightly.

Gretchen hung up the phone. Had she blown it with Parker? Maybe she didn't have as bad of luck with men as she'd thought. The credit check revealed Charlotte to be the best of the three potential renters. She called to tell her the good news.

Before she hung up, Gretchen asked, "I know this is odd, but would you mind giving me your brother's phone number?"

"Sure," Charlotte said. "It's not really odd. Women ask for his number all the time, but I think you'd be good for him." She rattled off the phone number before Gretchen had a chance to explain the situation between Parker and herself. "Hey, I've got to go, but I really appreciate you letting me rent your house."

"Of course," she said automatically. "I'll be in touch about a move-in date."

"Thanks." Charlotte hung up.

As soon as Gretchen ended the call with Charlotte, she ran home to call Parker. With her nosy co-workers on the other side of her cubicle wall, she didn't want to make such a personal call in the office.

She leaned against the railing on her front porch and dialed his number. The phone rang a few times and then went to voicemail. She hung up without leaving a message. She sat down on the flowered cushion of the wicker porch swing. Well, she'd tried to make amends. Her stomach twisted with more disappointment than she expected to feel. She pushed the swing back and forth a few inches. What was her next move? At this point, should she try to call him again, or drop it completely?

The quiet movement of the swing brought out the scent of the magnolias growing next to the porch. She inhaled the flowery aroma and exhaled slowly to quell her rising anxiety. She was getting too wrapped up in this.

A few minutes later, her phone vibrated its way across the swing cushion. She stared at the screen as if it were an alien life form. It was the same number she'd just called—Parker's number.

"Hello." She tapped her fingers on the wicker arm. She'd wanted to talk to him, so why was she so nervous?

"Hi." He sounded perplexed. "I got out of the shower

and saw you'd called. I didn't expect to hear from you again. Yesterday you acted like you wanted to forget we'd ever met."

Before she could stop herself, she imagined him standing with his phone pressed to his ear and wearing only a towel wrapped around his waist. Her heart beat faster.

"Uh, yes. Sorry about how I treated you at the house yesterday."

"Did I do something wrong?"

"No, it was me." Gretchen laughed nervously. "It's actually kind of a funny story." She paused. The circumstances suddenly seemed much more awkward than funny. "I thought you were married."

"Married? Why would you think that? We went out on a date."

"Well, you showed up at my house with Charlotte and the two of you were looking at the property together."

He laughed. "You thought I was Charlotte's husband? No wonder you gave me the cold shoulder."

"She never said you were her brother, and I just assumed." She sighed. "I'm really sorry about the misunderstanding." She hesitated and then pushed forward. "Would you be willing to let me make it up to you? We could have dinner tomorrow, my treat. I could come to Haven Shores if you'd like."

"I can't tomorrow night," he said. "I have a business meeting."

"Maybe Saturday night?"

"I'm sorry, I have another commitment on Saturday."

Her stomach sank. She'd screwed up any chance with him. Charlotte had said women asked for his phone number all the time. He probably already had dates scheduled with beautiful women for every night this week.

"That's okay. I understand," she said stiffly. "Please accept my apologies for my behavior yesterday." She pushed herself up from the swing, opened the front door, and let it bang closed behind her as she entered the living room.

"I can't on Friday or Saturday because I have work commitments, but how about tonight?" he asked. "I'm free tonight." His deep voice sent chills up her spine, stopping her mid-way through the living room.

"I'd love that." Tonight was sudden, but she could make it work. "Maybe Arturo's in Haven Shores for tapas at seven tonight?" she suggested. "I've heard good things about it from my co-workers. I'll make the reservation."

"Arturo's at seven it is. I'll see you there."

The phone clicked as he ended the call. Had she really just asked Parker out on a date? And he'd accepted? She did a little dance and then looked around. Reilly gave her an amused look and then put his head back down on the sofa.

She raced upstairs to figure out what to wear on her date. As she pulled a few possibilities out of her closet, she couldn't help feeling buoyantly happy. Things were looking up.

6

*T*he wooden door to Arturo's stood open slightly, allowing beats of jazz music to waft out. Gretchen touched the rough wood of the door, but hesitated before pulling on the wrought iron door handle. Insecurity stopped her from entering the restaurant. It had been a while since she'd been out on a real date. She couldn't back out now, even though she was pretty sure Parker was out of her league. She'd agreed to this date, and she owed him after the hard time she'd given him when he came to her house with Charlotte. A salt-filled breeze blew her hair back and fortified her resolve to enter. She smoothed down the hem of the little black dress she'd found at the back of her closet and entered the restaurant.

Inside, the lights were low and the chatter of patrons competed with the beats of the live jazz band. Delicious aromas floated in the air. Her co-workers had highly recommended Arturo's and raved about the tapas.

She didn't see Parker in the restaurant. She glanced at her watch. Ten until seven. She approached the hostess desk. "Hi, I have reservations for seven o'clock. Should be under Roberts."

The hostess checked her tablet. "Yes, I see you here."

"Has the other member of my party checked in yet?"

"No, not yet. Would you like to take a seat until they arrive?" The hostess motioned to a bench along the wall.

"Thanks." She settled herself on the bench next to a couple who were holding hands. Her stomach grumbled as she watched servers carry plate after plate of food out to the dining room. At exactly seven o'clock, Parker arrived.

"Hey," he said. "You look beautiful." He gave her a warm smile.

She smiled shyly in return and melted a little. "Thanks. You look nice yourself."

He was wearing a royal blue button-down shirt under a charcoal-gray suit that fit him like a glove. She hadn't thought he could improve on his looks from when she'd seen him last, but she'd been wrong.

The hostess noticed him and ran up to them with two menus in her hands. "I see the other member of your party has arrived." She beamed at Parker. "Right this way, sir."

Gretchen followed behind them to a table in the center of the restaurant. A votive candle flickered on the table. Parker pulled her chair out and then seated himself.

The hostess handed them their menus with another big smile for Parker. "Your server will be right with you."

He looked around the restaurant. "This place is nice. I hope the food tastes as good as it looks."

"Me too. I've been eying the shrimp since I got here," she admitted.

He opened his menu. "Well, let's get the shrimp then." He ran his finger down the menu options. "How about the clams and the gazpacho as well to start?"

"Perfect."

Their server arrived to take their drink and tapas orders. Gretchen ordered a Pinot Grigio and Parker asked for a glass of Merlot. After their drinks arrived, they sat and stared awkwardly at each other for a minute.

"So..." Gretchen started to say.

"Nice weather..." Parker said. They both laughed as they talked over each other and the ice was broken.

"Let's start over," he said. "Tell me about Candle Beach. Have you lived there a long time?"

"Yes, I grew up there. I moved away for college, but came back soon afterward." She sipped her wine and then set it back down on the coaster. "My whole family still lives there. In fact, the house that I live in, or rather that Charlotte will be living in, has been in my family since Candle Beach was founded in the early twentieth century."

"Ah, so your family is a founding family," he noted.

She laughed. "I guess you could say that. My grandfather's family used to come to Candle Beach for the summers to get out of the city. By the time my dad was born, the family lived there year-round. Have you lived in Haven Shores for long?"

"Same as you," he said. "I grew up there and most of my extended family still lives there."

"Do you have any other siblings?"

"Well, you met Charlotte, but I have an older brother, Graham, and an older sister, Claire, who lives in town with her family. We also have two younger brothers, Michael and William, who both live in Seattle."

"Wow, that is a big family. I only have one sibling, Lindsay, but I'm close to my cousin who lives in Candle Beach as well. I can't imagine growing up with so many brothers and sisters. I'm jealous."

"Don't be." Parker grinned. "As the middle boy, it seemed like I was always in trouble. Graham could never do any wrong in my parents' eyes and my other brothers were several years younger."

"And you couldn't possibly have deserved any of it." Gretchen smothered a grin.

"Of course not." He smirked. "I was the picture of innocence."

Their food arrived and they dug in.

"Okay, this is amazing. My friends were right." She bit into her second shrimp. The seafood had been bathed in an addictive tomato and garlic broth.

"No kidding. I can't believe I've never tried this place before."

They were finishing their first order of tapas and contemplating a second round when a buxom brunette wearing a strapless red dress approached the table.

"Parker!" she said. She leaned in to hug him, showing off a considerable amount of cleavage.

"Annabelle, nice to see you."

"It's been a while." She eyed him hungrily.

"It has," he said in a non-committal manner.

"Where have you been? I tried calling you, but you didn't pick up."

"Ah, things have been busy with work." He turned to Gretchen. "Gretchen, this is Annabelle, a family friend. Annabelle, this is Gretchen, my date."

Annabelle's face fell. "Well, I was just here having cock-tails with friends. Have fun on your little date." She leaned in to hug him again and whispered loudly, "I'll give you a call later."

His face reddened as she tossed her long hair back and

flounced off toward a group of women who had gathered by the door.

"A family friend, huh?" Gretchen teased.

"Yes, a friend of my brother's mainly, but I gave in and went out on a date with her a few months ago. Never again though. She's not the brightest tool in the shed."

Gretchen nodded, but worry niggled at her. If he usually dated women like Annabelle, how could she compete with that? "So, now that I know all about what a troublemaker you were as a child, why don't you tell me a little about grownup Parker? What do you do for work? Or for fun?"

"Well, for fun, I like to get outdoors, mainly hiking and camping. I also enjoy getting out on my family's fishing boat. It's nice to get out on the open ocean." A faraway look crossed his face. "After being around my family all day at work, it's refreshing to get away."

"I completely understand." Maybe they had more in common than she'd thought. "So you work in the family business?"

"Yes, Gray and Associates. It's a real estate company. We mainly sell properties in the Haven Shores area." He finished off his wine. "You may have seen the signs around town?"

"So you're a real estate agent," Gretchen said slowly. Unfortunately, she was very familiar with the Gray family, or rather, their reputation. She looked out the window. What were the odds that she'd end up on a date with the son of her parent's archenemies?

"Yes." He regarded her with an odd expression. "Why? Is that a problem?"

"No." She sighed. "In fact, we do have a lot in common. I'm also a real estate agent. My parents own Candle Beach Real Estate."

"Oh. That is a coincidence. So you're Eliza and Daniel Roberts' daughter." He fiddled with the stem of his empty wine glass. The server came over and motioned to the glass, but Parker covered the opening with his hand and shook his head. The server left as quickly as he'd appeared. "Do your parents still hate mine with a passion?"

Gretchen made a face. "Unfortunately, yes. They'd probably kill me if they knew I was out on a date with you." Her eyes darted around the restaurant. She hoped no one there recognized her or her date.

"It's been twenty years. You'd think they'd be over it by now. One bad real estate deal and they become mortal enemies."

"Uh-huh." She looked around the room again.

He stared at her. "Is this a problem for you? Who my parents are?"

Was it a problem that her parents would probably disown her if they found out she'd dated him? She didn't say anything for a moment. "I don't know." Since she was a teenager, she'd grown up with her parents bad-mouthing the Gray family and being hyper-competitive with them in the local real estate market.

The server came by to ask if they needed anything else. Gretchen's appetite had disappeared and she didn't want another round of tapas, so she said no. He brought their check to the table, along with some mints. She reached for the bill, but Parker picked it up and laid his credit card on the tray. The server whisked it away and then had him sign the receipt.

"Thank you," she said. "It's been a lovely dinner." He nodded understandingly.

She put her wrap on and followed him out of the restaurant.

They stood in front of the restaurant. Gretchen wasn't sure of the next move. She didn't want the date to end, but she also wasn't sure she wanted to face her parents if she started a romantic relationship with Parker Gray.

Parker cleared his throat. "Are you interested in taking a walk on the boardwalk?"

"Sure." Maybe more time with him would help her evaluate the situation.

They walked in silence over to the wooden boardwalk. After about a hundred feet, Parker stopped and leaned against the railing. Gretchen joined him and gazed out at the ocean. The temperature had chilled considerably and she pulled her lace wrap tighter against her cocktail length, spaghetti-strapped dress.

"Here," he said, removing his jacket. He placed it around her shoulders and pulled her closer. They stared out at the moonlit beach. Tufts of grass waved on the sandy dunes and the water shimmered in the glow of the moon. If it weren't for the tumultuous thoughts running through her mind, it would have been a magical, romantic evening.

Parker pulled away to face her.

"Look, I know we've got the family drama thing, but I really like you. I'd like to see where this can go." He peered into her eyes. "How are you feeling?"

She quieted the negative thoughts and allowed herself to really look at him. His gaze was intense and she felt herself drowning in his eyes.

"I'd like to see where this goes too," she said quietly. A shock of exhilaration and dread shot through her simultaneously. "Maybe we could keep it quiet for a while? Just to not stir the pot until we know for sure?"

"And not get to see our family's reactions?" he joked. "Think about what we'd be missing out on."

"I'm thinking about it, for sure. It would be quite explosive." She laughed quietly and her eyes met his. On his breath, she could smell the sweetness of the after dinner mint he'd consumed.

Without thinking, she stood on her tiptoes and leaned into him. He bent down and his lips met hers for a long kiss that made every nerve in her body tingle. They broke apart and he put his arm around her shoulder, pulling her close against his solid chest as they looked out to sea. Her eyes slid up to his face and she snuggled closer. If this was what every date with Parker would be like, a relationship with him would be worth her parents' wrath.

Too soon, she realized there were fewer and fewer people out on the boardwalk. She checked her watch and was disappointed to see it was close to ten o'clock. She still needed to prepare for her interview the next day.

"I'm so sorry, but I've got to get home. I have a big day tomorrow."

Parker checked his phone. "I should be getting home too." He took her hand in his and walked her to her car.

She unlocked the car and got in, but before she could close the door, Parker said, "Wait." She looked up at him. He stepped around the doorframe and leaned in to kiss her again. "Goodnight," he said softly.

"Goodnight," she whispered back. He closed the door and waved at her before getting into his own car.

She drove back to Candle Beach in a haze. Their date had contained so many ups and downs, from the great conversation at the restaurant, to Annabelle's intrusion, to the discovery of the feud between their families. And then that wonderful kiss on the boardwalk.

All in all, the date had exceeded her expectations. If she and Parker wanted to further their relationship, they'd have to face their parents. But they'd only had one date so far, so that distasteful task could be prolonged. With her track record, there was always the possibility that Parker may not be the man she thought he was, so she'd prefer to not tell her parents yet. She didn't think that would be the case, but you never knew.

7

*G*retchen set the hair dryer down on the bathroom counter and ran a brush through her brunette hair. She tugged at the tangles until her hair gleamed in waves that reached almost to the middle of her back. Some of that length needed to go before summer or she'd be miserable in the hot weather. *Bringg! Bringg!* Her phone vibrated along the tile and crashed into the hair dryer.

"Hello?" She didn't recognize the caller.

"Hi, this is Dory, calling from Martin Egglesby's office. I'm trying to reach Gretchen Roberts." The woman's breathless tones reminded her of the tinny voice used on the intercom at a popular women's clothing store.

"This is she." What now? Was her chance at the job over before it began?

"Oh, hi," the woman cooed. "I'm glad I caught you. Mr. Egglesby has had something come up and he won't be able to interview you today."

"Oh." She looked around the room. After coming home from her date with Parker, she'd stayed up late to compile her sales data and iron her interview clothing. Everything was wrinkle-free and ready for her big interview.

"He'd like me to reschedule your appointment. Does Monday at nine o'clock in the morning work for you?"

Gretchen grabbed her day planner and flipped to Monday. "Monday is great."

"Oh, wonderful. I'll let him know," the woman chirped. "Have a nice weekend."

"You too," she said automatically and hung up.

Well, at least she was dressed for work now. She called her office to let them know she'd be in after all.

After the excitement and high of preparing for her interview, returning to work felt like a letdown. She pushed through a mound of rental paperwork that had materialized on her desk. By lunchtime, she was itching to get out of the office. On a whim, she stopped in at To Be Read to see if Dahlia had time for lunch.

A teenager she didn't recognize was perched on the stool behind the bookstore's sales counter. Other than the girl, the store was empty.

"Good afternoon," the teenager said. "Is there anything I can help you find?"

"Actually, is Dahlia in? I'm a friend of hers."

"She's in the back." The girl pointed at the door. "Do you want me to get her?" Her face twisted with concern. "I'm not sure if I'm supposed to allow people to go back to her office."

"I think it would be fine, but yes, please let her know I'm here." Gretchen browsed the mystery aisle as the girl disappeared into the back room.

Dahlia came out of the back room with the girl in tow. She brought her over to where Gretchen waited, engrossed in reading the back of a book.

"Thank you, Emily," she said. Then she pointed to

Gretchen. "This is Gretchen, and it's fine to allow her to go into the back room. But I appreciate you checking with me first." Emily nodded and scurried back to the sales counter.

"So what's up?" Dahlia asked.

"I was dying at the office and needed to get out." She replaced the book on the shelf. "Do you have time for lunch?"

Her friend glanced at the clock behind the sales desk. "I can probably take a break. Let me check with Emily to see if she's okay manning the fort while I'm gone for an hour."

Dahlia chatted with the teenager, whose face held a mixture of apprehension and excitement.

"Alright," she said when she returned to Gretchen. "She's fine for now. It's probably a good idea to test her out alone for a short time while we're not as busy. When the tourist season starts up in a few weeks, she's going to need to be able to manage the bookstore herself some days."

"Does teriyaki sound good to you?" Gretchen asked, as they walked out the front door of the bookstore. "We could get Tasty Teriyaki."

"Yum. That does sound good. Can we get it to go?" Dahlia held her head up to the sun. "This has been a long winter and I want to soak up all the sun I can get while it's here."

Gretchen laughed. "Sure."

After they received their lunch orders, they took them to the Marina Park and sat on one of the benches facing the ocean.

"So," Gretchen began. "I went on a date with Parker." She sniffed her teriyaki and pulled a plastic fork out of the bag. The sweet and spicy steam wafting off of the food reminded her she was famished.

"Wait, Parker? The married guy? You went on a date

with a married guy?" Dahlia put down her takeout container and stared at her friend.

"Parker. The unmarried guy." Gretchen's eyes twinkled. This was kind of fun.

"I'm so confused."

"It turns out I was wrong. Parker wasn't Charlotte's husband. He's her brother."

"Whoa. That's like a soap-opera crazy turn of events." Dahlia sipped her soft drink through a straw. "So, spill. What was he like?"

"He was actually pretty great," Gretchen admitted. "We went to Arturo's in Haven Shores. The conversation was easy and he's not hard to look at." She stopped talking and frowned.

"But?" Dahlia stared at her friend. "What could be bad about any of that?"

"But he's Parker Gray," Gretchen finished.

"I don't understand. Who's Parker Gray?"

"Of Gray and Associates, the biggest real estate company on this part of the coast. They're based in Haven Shores."

"Okay," Dahlia said slowly. "I'm still not getting it. Isn't that a good thing? You must have so much in common."

"Unfortunately, we do. Our parents hate each other. Something about a real estate deal that went south twenty years ago."

"Seriously?" Dahlia said. "Who can hold a grudge that long?"

Gretchen shrugged. A napkin blew off the bench and Dahlia twisted around to pick it off the ground before the wind swept it away. When she looked up, consternation filled her face.

"Uh-oh." She closed her food container. "I think I see someone who can hold a grudge that long."

"What are you talking about?" Gretchen looked over her shoulder.

"Gretchen Elizabeth Roberts," Eliza Roberts scolded as she bore down on them.

Dahlia scooped up her food. "I'll see you later," she called as she escaped the path of Gretchen's mother.

All too quickly, Eliza was standing in front of the park bench. Gretchen put down her own food and closed up the box. The teriyaki suddenly smelled cloyingly sweet and her appetite vanished.

"Hey, Mom." Her lips quivered as she smiled at Eliza. How much did her mother know? There was no way she could have found out about Parker already, right? Was this about the real estate sales position? She'd expected her parents to be upset about that, but not this furious.

"Why am I hearing from Agnes Barnes that you were out with Parker Gray last night?" Eliza's eyes blazed and her hands were planted firmly on her hips.

Agnes Barnes? How did the most notorious gossip in Candle Beach find out about her date? Her fingernails dug into the takeout box. Was anything private in this town?

Her mother noticed her confusion. "She heard about it from a friend's daughter who ate at Arturo's last night."

Gretchen groaned.

"So, why were you out with Denise and Barry Gray's son last night?"

She had hoped to put this off for as long as possible and she certainly hadn't expected it to rear its ugly head within twenty-four hours of their date. She squirmed in her seat as her mother's eyes drilled holes into her skull.

Gretchen, get it together. You can date anyone you like, she counseled herself.

"Mom." She stopped. How best to explain this? "I met Parker last weekend at the chocolate festival. We hit it off and went out on a date yesterday evening. I had no idea who his parents were before then." In hindsight, she'd had a clue since she knew from the rental application that Charlotte's last name was Gray, but she hadn't put two and two together at the time.

Her mother continued to look at her with disapproval. "His parents are not good people. Your father and I do not approve of this relationship."

Gretchen had had it with her parents interfering in her love and professional life. And it wasn't like she planned to get married after only one date.

"Mom, I'm thirty-two years old. This is my life. Respectfully, you have no right to choose who I do or don't date. Parker seems like a nice man and I intend to get to know him better."

Until then, she hadn't realized how strongly she felt about a future relationship with him. The memories of their date the night before flooded back. The easy conversation and romantic kiss in the moonlight. She narrowed her eyes at her mother.

Eliza's face was stony. "This is a bad idea. If Parker Gray is anything like his parents, he can't be trusted. The apple doesn't fall far from the tree. For the record, I don't see this ending well." She left Gretchen alone on the bench with her uneaten lunch.

Gretchen sat for a moment, lost in thought. She hated disappointing her parents, but it was time that they realized she was an independent adult.

But was she? She lived in a house she'd inherited from her grandmother and she worked at the business her parents owned. She'd even allowed them to pigeonhole her into the property management side of the business although her heart led her to the sales side.

She walked over to a nearby garbage can and dumped the nearly full box of chicken teriyaki and rice into the gaping mouth of the metal can.

Her parents didn't spend much time in the office, but she wasn't taking any chances. Another conversation with her mother was not high on her to-do list. She ducked into Candle Beach Real Estate and rushed to her desk. She told her co-worker she wasn't feeling well and gathered what she needed to work from home for the rest of the day. Her laptop bag weighed heavily on her shoulder as she walked up the hill to her house.

She stopped in front of her Gram's house and stared at it. After next week, Charlotte would live there. It was weird to think about someone else living in Gram's house, but renting it out got her one step closer to being out from under her parents' thumb.

Reilly woke Gretchen early on Sunday morning by licking her face. She opened her eyes, expecting to see rain. Instead, sunlight peeked through the window shades. She drew the shades and stared at the ocean. When Charlotte moved in, she'd no longer wake up to this view. Might as well enjoy it now.

She brewed a small pot of coffee and took a cup outside to the porch. As she swung on the porch swing, she reflected on how glad she was that she'd be staying on the same property. She'd miss her neighbors and her gardens if she moved into an apartment in town. An icy chill shot through her. All of this would be lost when she moved to Seattle. *You've got to try something new,* she told herself. She couldn't stay in Candle Beach forever without a change.

One thing in her life had changed though—her budding romance with Parker. The unexpectedly beautiful weather gave her an idea. Although sunny, the March winds would be blowing fiercely down on the beach. She placed her coffee cup on the porch and dialed Parker's number.

"Hey," she said, when he answered. "It's me, Gretchen."

"Gretchen, hi."

She loved how her name rolled so smoothly off his tongue. She took a deep breath to settle her nerves. With meeting Parker and the upcoming interview for the sales position, she felt frazzled. But frazzled in a good way. At least that was what she told herself.

"I was wondering if you were busy today. I thought I could meet you in Haven Shores and we could fly kites on the beach. I have two older kites that I haven't used in a while." She held her breath waiting for him to respond.

"I'm not busy until early evening. Flying kites sounds fun," he said. She could hear his smile through the phone. "How about we meet at the main beach entrance at eleven? We can grab lunch afterward."

Gretchen agreed and ended the call. She leaned back, pushing the seat against the wall and then letting the momentum carry her back and forth. It was nice to have someone she could call on at the spur-of-a-moment for a fun date activity. She couldn't remember the last time she'd taken the kites out of storage.

Gretchen got to Haven Shores thirty minutes early. On the drive down, she'd passed Oceanview Estates. Now, butterflies of doubt flew around in her stomach. She wanted something hot to drink on the chilly beach, but coffee didn't sound good. No point in fueling her anxiety with more caffeine.

She stopped in at Starbucks for tea. Before ordering her drink, she visited the bathroom to freshen up before her date. Monkeys were dancing a jig inside her and she couldn't stop thinking about her interview the next day.

She peered at her reflection in the bathroom mirror. *It's going to be okay,* she told herself. A worried face stared back at her.

"Are you alright?" a woman in her late fifties asked. She wore tan linen slacks under a black sleeveless shift. Gretchen felt scrubby in comparison.

"I'm fine," she said. "Sorry, I was talking to myself."

"It sounded like you were worried about something," the woman observed. "Is there anything I can do to help? I have six kids of my own, so I have a lot of experience if you need a friendly ear."

Gretchen looked at her watch and then back at the woman. She didn't usually befriend strangers, but there was still twenty minutes before she needed to meet Parker. The woman smiled pleasantly at her. Maybe it would do her some good to talk with someone impartial about her interview nerves.

"I'd like that." They exited the bathroom and the woman found them a table while Gretchen ordered a mint tea. As she approached the woman with her drink, she again wondered what she was doing. This woman was a stranger to her. In some respects, that seemed better because she'd most likely never see her again. She sat down at the table and sipped her tea.

The woman smiled at her. "So what's going on?" she asked.

"I have this job interview tomorrow and I can't get it out of my head that I'm going to screw it up."

"I'm sure you aren't going to screw it up. Is it an interview for a position you have experience in?"

"Yes, well, no. I don't know how to answer that." Gretchen slumped. "It's for the sales position at a new development up the coast. Anyways, I have experience in property management, but not really in real estate sales."

Her companion opened her mouth to say something and then shut it before uttering a word.

Gretchen noticed the woman's hesitation and said quickly, "I'm a licensed real estate agent, I just haven't had many opportunities to sell properties."

The woman nodded. "If this is something you're interested in, you should pursue it. You can't get experience in something if you aren't actively doing it."

That made a lot of sense to Gretchen. She finished her tea, savoring the strong hit of mint from the bottom of the cup. What time was it? She glanced at the clock on the wall and pushed her chair away from the table. "I've got to go meet someone, but I really appreciate the advice. You've made me feel a lot better."

The woman regarded her with a contented smile. "I'm glad I could help. Hey, I never got your name."

"Gretchen Roberts."

The woman's smile slipped for a moment and then reappeared. "Nice to meet you. Good luck with your interview."

Gretchen thanked her and hurried out to her car. She arrived at the beach parking lot just as Parker pulled up.

He grinned at her and jogged over to her car, where he

helped her retrieve the kites from her car. "This was a great idea. I'm glad you thought of it."

"Me too." Between her conversation with the woman and Parker's companionship, her spirits were rising as high as the kites being flown on the beach. Things were going to work out.

_____

8

"Parker, are you there?" a woman's voice called from the other side of the door to his condo. She knocked again. He'd tried to ignore the knocking, but she wasn't going to give up. He turned off the TV and ambled to the front door.

"I'll be there in a second." The knocking stopped.

He opened the door. "Hi, Mom."

Denise Gray pushed past him into the kitchen, flipping on the lights as she went. "This place is so dark. I don't know how you live like this."

He winced at the abrupt change in light. "I was watching TV."

"You need to get out of the house, meet a nice girl."

"Yes, Mom." He certainly wasn't going to tell her that he'd spent the day flying kites at the beach with a nice girl. He wasn't ready to tell her about Gretchen yet.

Even though he'd sworn off women, there was something about Gretchen that had immediately attracted him to her. The day they met, he couldn't help asking her out to lunch at the Bluebonnet Café. Their romantic date at

Arturo's had solidified the feeling. She was different. If his mother got her hooks into his relationship with Gretchen, she'd make a mess of it.

Denise sat down on a bar stool and tapped her foot against the metal rung.

"What?" he asked. She had that look on her face like she was bursting to tell him something.

"You'll never guess who I met today."

"Who? Queen Victoria?" He crossed his arms over his chest and leaned against the refrigerator.

"No. Gretchen Roberts." She regarded him with a smug expression on her face.

"Gretchen Roberts," he repeated. How had his mother found out already about them dating? To hide his stunned reaction, he turned and grabbed a glass out of the cupboard and filled it from the refrigerator's water tap.

"Yes, Eliza and Daniel Roberts' daughter. Apparently she followed them into the family business. Probably just as crooked as they are. She was in Starbucks this morning and was telling me about how she was in the running for the Oceanview Estates job."

"Really." Her comment about Gretchen had caused his blood pressure to rise. She didn't even know Gretchen and she was making assumptions about her. He wanted to defend her, but if he did so, it would reveal their relationship and he wanted to keep it quiet for a little longer.

"Yes. And get this: she's worried about not being a good candidate for it. You should try to get the position instead. You'd be perfect for it." Denise pulled her phone out of her purse. "Your father and I met Martin Egglesby last month at a real estate developer's conference. If you're interested, I can call him now and let him know." She stared at him, waiting for his response.

His head spun with the news, but he tried hard not to let it show. At least she didn't seem to know that Gretchen had been in Haven Shores to meet him. He sipped his water.

"Thanks for the offer, but I don't need you to arrange an interview for me. I can get jobs on my own." He walked over to the door and opened it.

Denise took the hint. As she brushed past him, she put her hand on his arm. "I know things have been tough for you with Graham lately. This type of opportunity could be a huge boost to your career—and for Gray and Associates. Just think about it." She left, the scent of her floral perfume trailing after her.

He returned to his seat on the couch and picked up the remote, but didn't turn the TV back on. His mother was right. The position at the new development could thrust his career forward. But was it worth it to go head-to-head with Gretchen to achieve that goal?

On Monday morning, Gretchen dressed in her most professional blouse and skirt, drank her coffee and forced herself to eat a piece of buttered toast. She normally ate a larger breakfast, but the churning in her stomach made her rethink that this morning. Her interview with Martin could be one of the most important events in her life. If she was hired to sell the properties, she would have the experience necessary to make it in a bigger city. Maybe he'd even hire her for another project. This was huge.

At the thought of moving to another city, she flashed back to her date with Parker. If she moved away from the area, she'd be leaving Parker. She brushed the thought aside. Although her date with him on Thursday night had been magical, they'd only had one date, two if you counted lunch at the Bluebonnet Café after the chocolate festival. She'd worry later about how moving would affect her relationship with him.

She removed her suit jacket from the hanger and pushed her arms through the sleeves, then checked out her reflection in the mirror. Her wavy, dark hair was pulled back into a sensible bun, and no dog hairs sullied the gray suit jacket and skirt. The turquoise shirt highlighted the blue in her eyes and brightened her pale complexion.

"You're going to rock this interview," she said confidently into the mirror. "You're a professional." The woman in the mirror smiled back at her.

She recited positive affirmations while she drove the few miles to her interview. A business and self-improvement book she'd once read had advised visualizations and affirmations before important business meetings, and she'd found that they helped to center her.

She parked in front of the sales office trailer and took a few deep, calming breaths. Then she checked her face in the mirror and stepped out of the car. Straightening her skirt, she picked her way across the graveled parking lot in her kitten heels. With another deep breath, she knocked on the door.

"Come in," a voice boomed from inside.

The older man she'd seen when she met Maggie at Off the Vine sat behind a desk. He motioned to the seat across from him.

"Gretchen, I presume."

She nodded. The scent of cinnamon air freshener filled the air and she fought the urge to sneeze.

"Please, sit down." He smiled at her. "Can I get you anything? A glass of water?"

"No, I'm fine." She sat, clutching a black portfolio. Her heart beat fast with nerves and she figured she'd be more likely to spill the water on herself than drink it.

"Let's get started then."

She released her tight grip on the portfolio and removed sales data from the properties she'd sold. She handed it to him. He flipped through the pages, but didn't look impressed.

"It appears that you've sold a few individual properties, but I don't see any experience as the primary real estate agent on a new development." He peered at her from over the top of his glasses. "I was under the impression that you had more experience. Your friend, Maggie, said you'd been working as a real estate agent at Candle Beach Real Estate for ten years."

"I apologize if Maggie gave you a false impression of my work history," Gretchen said. What exactly had Maggie told him?

"Well, is it true?" He leaned back in his chair and crossed his arms.

"Yes, I've worked there for ten years. It's only been in the last few years that I obtained my real estate license and I've mainly worked on the property management side. Maggie knew I'd worked there for that time, but she may not have known the details of my job responsibilities." She had a sinking feeling in the pit of her stomach. He was obviously annoyed that his time had been wasted.

Maggie had a tendency to look on the bright side of situations and see the best in people. She hadn't meant to give Martin the wrong idea, but she'd twisted the facts to present Gretchen in the best possible light. Now, it was Gretchen's turn to take the opportunity she'd been given and run with it.

"No, I haven't sold a new development like this," she admitted. "But I welcome the chance to do so. Candle Beach doesn't often have developments of this magnitude and I'm very excited about it. This will help drive other developments on the coast and I want to help make the project a success. Any new business brings tourist dollars to Candle Beach."

"Can you tell me what your best qualities are as a salesperson?" He picked up the stapled documents she'd given him and rifled through them again.

"I'm driven, I'm a people person, and most of all I want to help clients find the best house for their needs. A house is the largest purchase most people will ever make and I want to be a part of that process."

"Good answer." He smiled and ran his finger along the corners of the paper. "I'm still concerned about your lack of experience though. As you said, this is a big development and I need to make sure whoever we choose is well suited for the job."

She nodded. "I know I can handle the responsibility."

She wasn't sure she was the most qualified person for the job based on experience, but she could handle the role and he wouldn't find anyone more focused on the client's needs. Working as a property manager for the last ten years had given her the ability to understand what a client really needed and to anticipate things that they didn't even know they wanted. Until that moment, she hadn't realized how much she really wanted to be the primary real estate agent at the new development.

She pushed her feet into the floor and sat up straight. Looking directly into his eyes, she said, "If you hire me to sell here, you won't be sorry."

He smiled and set his reading glasses on the desk. "I

appreciate your optimism and drive." He stood and she followed suit, gathering her belongings.

"I'll be in touch after I make a decision. I'm interviewing a few other agents for the role, but I should know something by tomorrow."

She thanked him and retreated from the office, pushing the door closed behind her with a resounding click. In the parking lot, she didn't know whether to laugh or cry. The interview could have gone better, but she didn't know what else she could have done to convince him to hire her.

Another car had parked across from her, but she didn't see anyone around. As she reached into her purse to pull out her car keys, the car's door slammed. The sun obscured her vision and she had to shade her eyes to see who had gotten out. When the person came into focus, she was thankful she hadn't laughed or cried.

"Parker." Gretchen's face lit up. After the disappointing interview, she was happy to see a familiar face. "What a nice surprise. I didn't expect to see you." She hugged him and then stepped back. "How did you know I was here?"

Parker's face reddened and he shifted his weight from foot to foot.

"Um," he said. "I didn't know you were going to be here." Uncharacteristic nervousness flitted across his eyes.

She stepped back further to assess him. If possible, he was dressed even nicer than he had been for their date on Thursday night.

"Why are you here then?" She feared she already knew the answer to her question, but she needed him to say it.

"I'm interviewing for the role of the real estate agent for

the project." He cocked his head to the side. "I'm assuming you're here for the same reason?"

"Yes," she said in a tight voice. Her heart sank. "We just completed my interview for it."

"Gretchen, I'm so sorry," Parker said. "This is such a crazy situation. Believe me, if I could change things, I would."

"You didn't think to mention on Thursday that you'd be interviewing for this job?" She hadn't realized before how small the real estate community actually was in their coastal region. What were the odds that she'd be up against Parker for a job soon after they met?

"It didn't seem relevant to our conversation. And to be fair, you never mentioned you were up for the job either." He ran his fingers through his hair.

"I'm sure you didn't know anything about it," Gretchen said sarcastically. Her mother had been right about Parker. Whoever was chosen for the sales position would earn a sizable amount of commissions. Had he only feigned interest in her to assess the competition?

"How would I know then that you'd be here today? With all the drama regarding our parents, we didn't talk much about work." He edged toward the door. "I need to get in there, but I hope we can talk about this later. I'll call you tonight, okay?" He clapped her on the shoulder.

She said nothing. Was he telling her the truth? What was the proper thing to say in this situation? She didn't wish him ill, but saying 'good luck' seemed an odd sentiment if it meant him getting the role over her. But she had to say something.

"I hope your interview goes well. He was very nice," she eked out.

He nodded. "Thank you. I'm sure you did a great job in there too."

She quickly got into her car and slammed the door before driving off in a cloud of dust.

Parker watched Gretchen drive away. When she'd realized why he was there, her face had crumpled like he'd stomped all over her with hiking boots.

Should he have told her he was her competition prior to her interview? He hated lying to her, but he knew telling her about his conversation with his mother would be a bad idea. It would only hurt her to know his mother had betrayed her. But this had all happened at the worst possible time.

Now, not only did they have to contend with parents that feuded like the Montagues and Capulets, they had this wrench thrown into the mix. One of them may win the role of primary real estate agent for the development, but no one would truly win. The tension created by this could ruin their budding relationship.

He didn't want that to happen. If it weren't for the fact that he needed this job to show everyone he was ready to break away from the family business, he would concede the position. It was obvious that Gretchen badly wanted the job.

He threw his head back and swore under his breath. Finally, he'd met a woman who challenged and interested him. Now this. Why on earth did they both have to have the same profession? He ran his hand through his hair and composed himself. He'd have to try to act like nothing had happened, or he'd have no chance of earning the job himself.

9

*G*retchen had been looking forward to a brunch date with her friends, but now she dreaded seeing Maggie after the debacle with Martin earlier in the day. She knew Maggie hadn't meant any harm by talking her up to him, but the interview had been an embarrassment.

When she arrived at the Bluebonnet Café, Maggie and Dahlia were already deep in conversation and had ordered a round of coffee for the three of them.

"Hey guys." Gretchen gave them each a quick hug. "I'm so glad we were able to get together. Things have been crazy at work."

"At the bookstore too," Dahlia said. "I guess I can't complain. Last year at this time, I was begging for sales."

Maggie nodded. "I love this time of year—for the tourists, and because it's finally warming up. That's one thing I liked about living on base in Southern California. It was always sunny there, no matter what time of year."

The waitress came by and they placed their orders.

Maggie turned to Gretchen. "Hey. How did your interview go?"

"Yeah, about that." Gretchen tried to scowl at Maggie, but it came out as a lopsided grin.

"What did I do?" Maggie asked, the picture of innocence.

"You told Martin Egglesby that I had ten years of real estate sales experience."

"I did not!" Maggie exclaimed. She flushed from the V of her purple blouse all the way to the roots of her fiery red hair.

Gretchen gave her the eye.

"Okay, okay. I may have enhanced your resume a bit. But you deserve it. You're great at what you do and I know you'd be awesome at that job."

"Well, I don't think he felt the same way." Gretchen squirted ketchup onto her eggs and smeared it around. Making a mess of her food was oddly satisfying.

"So you haven't heard anything from him yet?" Maggie asked as she dug into her strawberry-covered waffles.

"No, nothing. I don't expect to hear anything until tomorrow at the earliest." She stirred cream into her coffee and then set the spoon down on the table. "Oh, and get this. The other candidate he interviewed was Parker Gray." She brought the mug of coffee to her mouth and blew on it, causing the remaining blotches of cream to swirl. Steam rose up and tickled her nose. It was still too hot to drink, so she set it down.

"Parker Gray? As in the married yet unmarried guy you went out with?" Dahlia asked. "Well, there's one thing to say about him—he's full of surprises."

Maggie nodded. "No kidding. Did you know beforehand that he'd be there too?"

"No." Gretchen leaned her elbows on the table and put

her chin in her hands. "I had no idea. He said he didn't know either. I don't know what to believe. There seems to be a lot I don't know about him."

"Don't worry, Gretchen," Dahlia said. "I'm sure you've got this."

"I'm up against Parker Gray. He has so much more experience as a real estate agent than I do. Most of what I've done has been property management with a few sales on the side. I'm never going be able to compete." Gretchen slumped in her chair.

"Suck it up, buttercup," Dahlia quipped. "I didn't know anything about running a bookstore when I arrived in Candle Beach last year and now it's like I was born to be a bookstore owner."

"Yeah, but you owned the store and had control over it. I've argued with my parents for years to allow me to take a more active role in the sales part of the business, but they've always insisted my skills lay in property management."

"You are pretty calm dealing with the tenants and all of their crazy requests," Maggie said. Dahlia nodded in agreement.

"But property management is never going to get me any closer to my goals. I want to move to Seattle. For that, I'll need the big commissions, not just an hourly wage." She drank her cooled coffee and pushed a link sausage around the plate. "It seems hopeless."

"It's not hopeless." Maggie leaned forward. "The developer hasn't made a decision, right? Is there anything you can do to convince him you're the best candidate?"

Gretchen was about to reply when her phone rang. She checked the caller ID. Parker again. It was the fifth time he'd called her since they'd seen each other at the sales office. She placed her phone face down on the table.

"Who was that?" Dahlia asked before biting into her third piece of bacon.

"Parker," Gretchen answered. "He keeps calling."

"Maybe you should let him explain," Maggie said. "You said he didn't know you were interviewing for the job too. Maybe it's all a big misunderstanding."

"I don't know." Gretchen sighed. "The more I think about it, the more I realize what a mistake a relationship with him would be. There's always going to be things like this that come up. And with the animosity between our families, anything between us was doomed from the start."

"I think you're wrong," Dahlia said. "You said he was great. Now you're giving up at the first hint of trouble." She stared at Gretchen, who squirmed under her scrutiny.

"I want to move out of this town and start afresh. I'm not sure how Parker fits into that. It's probably best to nip the relationship in the bud now, before it gets serious." She turned to Maggie. "To answer your question, no. There's nothing I can do to change the developer's mind. I've already showed him my sales figures and anything else I can think of."

"You'll think of something," Maggie said, always the optimist. "Also, I agree with Dahlia. You and Parker looked perfect together when I saw you at the café."

"Let's talk about something else." Gretchen turned to Dahlia. "Like your wedding. When do we find out what our bridesmaid dresses are going to look like?"

Dahlia launched into a long description of the bridesmaid dress design. Gretchen did her best to appear interested, but her mind was far away from their cozy brunch. Her phone rang again. Parker. She held her hand over the button to send it to voicemail.

Maggie noticed her distraction. "Is that Parker again?"

Gretchen nodded. "Yeah, but I'm not going to answer it."

"Answer it!" Dahlia ordered.

"Just do it." Maggie stared her down.

Giving in to her friends' demands, she took a deep breath and answered Parker's phone call, but it was too late. The screen had gone blank.

"It already went to voicemail." A little part of her felt relieved to have dodged his call, but she knew that the longer she put it off, the more awkward it would be when they finally connected.

Maggie and Dahlia's faces fell.

"You could call him back," Maggie said.

"No, I'm not going to play phone tag." Gretchen paid her share of the bill with cash. "Girls, I'm tired and my head hurts. I think I'm going to go home for a while.

"Okay," they both said in unison, and Gretchen walked slowly toward the door.

"I'll call you later," Maggie called after her. Gretchen nodded to show she'd heard and exited the building.

Her head throbbed the whole way home. As she let herself into her house, her phone rang. A thrill shot through her. Parker had called her back. They could finally stop playing phone tag and get this mess straightened out. She pulled her phone out of her pocket.

It wasn't Parker.

"Ms. Roberts?" the man asked. "This is Martin Egglesby. How are you doing?"

"I'm fine. How are you?" she asked automatically. Her heart beat double time. This was it. Her life-changing moment.

"I'm fine, thank you. The reason I'm calling is that I've decided to offer the sales position to the other candidate I interviewed."

"Oh." She leaned against her front door. The pounding in her head increased.

"It was a pleasure to meet you, but I had to go with the other candidate as they had more experience."

She had been so close to her path to freedom and she'd let the job slip away. Could this be it? Was she doomed to stay in Candle Beach forever?

"Mr. Egglesby," she said. "Have you offered the job to the other person yet?"

"No, I called you first." He cleared his throat. "Why do you ask?"

"I'd like for you to give me another chance. Let me prove to you that I'm the best choice. I can sell more houses for you, quicker than anyone else."

He chuckled. "I like your moxie." He paused. "Tell you what, work up a presentation for me tomorrow that will blow my socks off. If I like it, the job is yours."

He spoke to someone off the line and then said, "I'm free at eleven a.m. tomorrow."

"Eleven o'clock it is. See you then." She pumped her fist in the air and silently shouted *yes*. "And Mr. Egglesby, you won't be disappointed."

"I hope not." He hung up the phone.

She stood in her living room, frozen in place. What had she just committed to? Parker had so much more sales experience than she had, but she'd just promised Martin that she was the best candidate for the job. What on earth had she done?

She flung herself on the couch and stared up at the ceiling. It was going to take some creative storytelling to make herself appear more qualified than Parker.

10

*S*omeone knocked on the front door. Gretchen pushed herself off the couch and opened the door. A cloud of rose and gardenia perfume wafted into the room.

"Mom." She stepped onto the porch and shut the door behind her.

"You act as though I never come and visit you at home. Can I come in?" Eliza Roberts looked pointedly at the closed door.

"It has been a while." In truth, it had been at least a year since her mother had been in her house. Eliza generally preferred to meet at a restaurant in town or have her daughter over to her house for family dinners. Gretchen opened the door and motioned to the inside of the house. "Uh, sure. Come in. It's a little messy in here."

Her mother sat primly on the couch and surveyed the room. "What's with all the boxes and packing tape?" She gestured to the stacks of boxes piled against the wall and the other moving materials Gretchen had left on an end table.

Shoot. Gretchen hadn't intended for her mom to find out this way that she was moving out of the main house. Not that it was any of her business. Grams had left her the house and she could do with it whatever she wanted. It was more that she didn't want to have to tell her mom the reason for moving out. She surreptitiously moved the folder with her resume and sales information off of the end table and stuck them in a drawer.

"I'm moving into the carriage house for a while." She edged over toward the door and pushed it opened a crack. Maybe her mom would take the hint and leave.

"Why?" Her mother's face twisted in confusion. "Are you painting the walls? I always thought this place could use a paint job. Have you thought about a cheery yellow? It would brighten up this room."

"No, I'm not painting," Gretchen said. "I've decided to rent my house out for the tourist season. There are so many tourists here for the summer that I might as well earn some money off of them if I have to deal with them every day."

"So you're listing it in the nightly rental pool?"

"No, I found someone who will be renting it on a monthly basis." She jutted out her chin. "She's very nice. I didn't need this much space anyways."

Her mother looked at her with suspicion. "Do you need money? Are you in trouble? Is it credit card debt?"

"No! I'm not in trouble. Why would you think that?"

"I don't know. You love this house and you've been so distant lately. Your father and I have invited you over for dinner every Sunday and you haven't accepted in weeks."

"I've been busy." She pointed to the boxes. "I've got to finish packing. You should probably go." She pushed the door open further.

"I'll help you." Her mother got to her feet and walked briskly over to the end table. She grabbed the packing tape dispenser, unfolded a box and laid a line of tape across the bottom. "What should I pack in here?"

Gretchen sighed and allowed the front door to close. Her mother was a force of nature. In truth, she did have a lot to pack before Charlotte arrived the next day and she could use the assistance.

"You can help pack up the kitchen. Follow me." She showed her mom the items to pack first. "I'm leaving the furniture, but everything else needs to go in boxes. I've already removed everything I'll need in the carriage house."

They packed for two hours, only speaking a few words to each other now and then.

"Gretchen," her mother finally said, hesitantly. "Why are you really moving out of the big house?"

Gretchen stopped what she was doing. Should she confide in her? Her parents had never understood before that she needed her independence. They'd always thought they knew best.

"I want to move to Seattle." There, she'd said it out loud. She peeked at her mother over the glass dish she'd been wrapping.

"Seattle? Why?" She looked puzzled. "All of your family and friends are here. Your job, your house. Why would you want to move?"

"That's exactly why. Something is missing from here. I've never experienced much more of the world than Candle Beach." She set the dish in the box. "I've always worked for you guys and never been out on my own."

"You went to college out of state," Eliza said. "You were on your own then."

"It's not the same thing." How could she explain this? "At college, I was still dependent on you for some money and everything was laid out for me—where I'd live, eat, and study. Then I came back here and fell into the same situation. I work for you and Dad, and I live in a house that belonged to my grandmother. I need to figure some things out on my own."

"Okay," her mother said slowly. "So what kind of job are you going to look for in Seattle?"

"I want to stay in real estate. I love real estate." She paused and looked directly into her eyes. "But I don't want to be a property manager anymore."

"I don't understand." Her mother set down a pile of utensils in a box. "We thought you loved your job. You're so good at it. All the tourists rave about how helpful you are."

"I do like my job, but it's not my dream."

"How are you going to find clients in Seattle? Do you have contacts there?" Worry lines wrinkled her face.

"There's this job..." Gretchen began.

"Where? In Seattle?" Her mother pushed herself to standing and arched her back to stretch it.

"No, in Candle Beach. Well, just down the road. It's that new development a few miles south of town—Oceanview Estates."

Her mother nodded. "I know what you're talking about. Your father and I thought about trying for the job, but we're already stretched so thin with tourist season coming up." She picked up the box she'd packed and stacked it against the corner.

"Right. If I get the job, think of the commissions I'd make. Not only that, but the owner, Martin Egglesby, owns several other developments all over the Northwest." Gretchen beamed with enthusiasm. "Think of all the opportunities for me that this could create."

"But wait, I heard through the grapevine that someone from Gray and Associates was a shoo-in for the job."

Gretchen grimaced. "Unfortunately, you heard correctly."

Her mother ran water into the teakettle and set it on the stove. "Aren't you dating one of the Gray boys?"

"Yes, Parker Gray," she said tersely. She removed two mugs from the cupboard. "And he's the other person being considered for the job."

"Oh." Eliza was quiet for a moment. "So what does that mean for you? Wouldn't it be strange to be in competition with each other?"

"It's not a problem," Gretchen said. "I broke it off with him." Well, she hadn't done so yet, but it was on her agenda for the next day. She watched steam shoot out of the teakettle and wished for it to be ready to pour—anything to take her mind off of Parker. As if by her command, the teakettle whistled.

"I'm sorry about Parker." Her mom handed her a teabag and poured the boiling water into the mugs.

"You made it quite clear that you disapproved of a relationship between Parker and me."

"True, but I still don't like to see you hurting."

She shrugged. "It's okay. I knew it wouldn't work out. I have to focus on getting the job."

"I'm sure the developer will see how great you are." Eliza dunked her teabag in the water.

Gretchen sat down in one of the two kitchen chairs. She brought the tea cup to her mouth, but it was too hot to drink.

"Actually, he called right before you arrived and told me he plans to give Parker the job."

"What?" her mother said. "Why?"

"He thinks Parker is better qualified than I am." She blew on the tea, sending tendrils of steam dancing into the air. "And he's probably right. Parker has years more sales experience than I do."

"That's probably our fault," her mother said. "We thought you liked managing the properties and didn't want the stress of sales."

"No, it always seemed exciting to me, but you never wanted me to move into that role." She leaned back in the chair. "It doesn't matter. What matters is that I asked Martin to give me another chance. At eleven o'clock tomorrow morning I have to somehow prove to him that I'm better than Parker Gray."

"Well, you're the best property manager we have. I wasn't kidding. The tourists love you. Can you use that to prove you're the best choice?"

"It's all I've got." Gretchen sighed. "I can't magically give myself more sales experience overnight, so I've got to use the skills I already have. If I don't get this job, I don't know what I'm going to do."

"Oh honey, I'm so sorry. We didn't know you felt this way. Next time we get a new client, I'll have your father refer them to you." Eliza's mouth turned down and her eyes were bright with tears.

"Mom, it's not even about that anymore." Gretchen moved over to hug her. She pulled back and looked into her mother's eyes. "I need to do something for me. I can't work for the family business much longer. Maybe sometime in the future I can come back, but for now, I need to be independent. Please understand."

"Okay. But honey, please let us know if there's anything we can do to help. We'd be happy to prepare a reference for you if it would help." Eliza dabbed at her eyes with a tissue. "We don't want you to go, but both of us want you to be happy. It's all we ever wanted. Please know that."

"I do." Gretchen hugged her again and then surveyed the room. "There's a lot of stuff left to pack. If I'm going to have enough time to prepare a presentation good enough to convince Martin to hire me, we'll need to hurry."

Eliza laughed and wiped her eyes again before picking up her tape dispenser. "Lead the way."

Gretchen sat in her car in front of the sales office and took ten deep breaths. This was the biggest moment of her life. If she failed, it was back to Candle Beach Real Estate. Although her mother had promised her she could become more involved with the real estate sales part of the business, she knew it wouldn't be the same as having a major sales role for a new residential subdivision.

Raindrops fell on her face as she stepped out of the car. Dark thunderclouds threatened to dump buckets of water on her if she didn't get inside soon. She held her raincoat hood tightly against her face to avoid messing up her hair and ran for the building. Under the overhang, she paused for a moment to collect her thoughts. When ready, she removed her jacket and hung it over her arm.

She ducked her head inside the sales trailer. "Mr. Egglesby?"

"Come in, come in. Please, call me Martin." He folded his hands in front of him and stared at her expectantly. "Have you come to wow me?"

"I hope so," she said brightly. She pulled out a file with comments left by past clients. "You're right that I don't have as much sales experience as other candidates. But what I do have is a passion for this. I will do whatever it takes to make sure that a customer has the best experience possible when they work on a home deal here. I want people to love their new home. That is something not everyone can offer."

She held out a piece of paper from her folder. "These are comments from some of the customers I've worked with in the past. I've never had a customer that was dissatisfied with my work."

He set his glasses on his nose and scanned the document.

"Impressive. I can see that you really care about your work in property management. But what makes you think that you'd be good at real estate sales?"

She took a deep breath. "Because I'll work twice as hard as anyone else to make the sale. I can work nights, weekends, anytime really. I want to show you how dedicated I am." She glanced at the positive comments she'd received in the past. Strengthened by the support of her clients, she stared straight into Martin's eyes. "You won't be disappointed in me."

"Well, thank you," he said. "You've given me a lot to think about."

She smiled at him. "Thank *you* for the opportunity."

He smiled back at her and nodded. They shook hands and said goodbye to each other.

She closed the door behind her and leaned against it. The thunderstorm had passed, leaving behind the acrid scent of recent rain. She stared up at the sun that peeked through the clouds. She'd done it. Only time would tell if Martin wanted to hire her, but she'd presented herself confidently. She was one step closer to realizing her dream of moving to Seattle.

"Gretchen," a man called out.

She lowered her focus from the sunny skies with a sense of déjà vu. "Parker."

He smiled at her and didn't seem to notice the icy quality of her voice. "I'm so glad to see you. You didn't give me a chance to explain earlier."

"What do you have there?" She pointed to the plastic bag he held in his hands. It was emblazoned with the Gray and Associates logo.

He had the good grace to blush. "Uh, just a few things I brought by for Martin."

She stalked over to him and tugged the bag open. It was filled with one of Parker's business cards and some measuring tapes with the Gray and Associates logo. They were nestled snugly against a bottle of liquor.

"You brought him Scotch?" she accused. The good ole boy network was alive and well.

He shrugged. "He mentioned in our interview that he enjoyed it, so I figured I'd bring him a bottle."

Her eyes narrowed. "So you're bribing him."

"No, I'm not bribing him. I'm giving him a bottle of Scotch. It's a common business practice." He sighed. "Look Gretchen, we both want this job. This is business, nothing else."

She stared at him, openmouthed. Was their situation really that black and white to him?

"I'm sorry," he said. "We both have our reasons for wanting this job, but only one of us will be chosen. If the other candidate had been someone else, I'd do the same thing. You haven't exactly given me a reason to treat you any differently than anyone else." He pointed to the phone she held in her hand. "I've called at least five or six times."

"Yeah, well, don't bother calling again," she said. "I'm not going to answer." Heat traveled up her neck and flushed her face. She gripped her phone in one hand and clenched her other fist. How could he say she was just like anyone else?

Now, more than anything, she wanted the job. Not to have the job itself, although that would be nice, but she wanted to beat Parker Gray. She turned on her heels, beeped her car to unlock it and drove away.

She fumed about Parker the whole way home. When she pulled into her driveway, a familiar car was parked in the alley spot furthest from the carriage house.

11

*G*retchen walked over to the big house and let herself in via the unlocked back door.

"I found the key you left me under the mat." Charlotte tossed the key in the air and caught it in her palm.

Gretchen nodded. "Glad you were able to get in while I was out." Charlotte had opened the windows for ventilation and fresh air circulated throughout the house, bringing with it the scent of magnolia blossoms. Gretchen glanced around the room. Some paintings leaned against the wall and stacks of boxes were piled in the middle of the floor. "Did all of these fit in your car?" If so, she must be a master packer. Her sedan wasn't that big.

"Yes," Charlotte laughed. "Overpacking cars is my superpower." She leaned over to open a box and removed some knickknacks, which she set on the end table. "I've moved in all my clothes and linens upstairs already. I don't have much stuff. Most of my money is tied up in the store."

"The store?" She wasn't aware that her new tenant owned a store.

"Yes, I thought I told you." Charlotte looked at her and

shook her head. "Sorry, sometimes I can be a space case. Have you seen the Airstream trailer parked downtown in the empty lot next to Pete's Pizzeria?"

"I have, why?" She'd figured the Airstream belonged to a local business owner and they'd parked it there until they could find a better place to store it.

"That's my new shop. I'll be selling out of the Airstream —mainly gift items and other fun stuff, but some of my art too. It'll be called 'Whimsical Delights.' Isn't that a great name? My sister thought it up."

"It's great." Now that she thought about it, she had noticed the Airstream being polished and new flowers planted outside of it. She'd been so wrapped up in her own problems that she hadn't given it another thought. "So is this a new business?"

Charlotte beamed. "Kind of, kind of not. I'd been selling my art out of a shop in Haven Shores and I decided that I wanted to have more control over where I sold from. So I bought the Airstream and moved up here."

"That's fantastic. I'm happy for you." Charlotte had done exactly what she hoped to do herself, although in a different industry and opposite locale. She gazed at the paintings propped against the wall. An ocean scene caught her eye. Even sideways, it was beautiful. "Is that one of yours?" She nodded at the canvas.

"It is," Charlotte said. "One of my earlier works. Not as advanced as the technique I now use, but there's something about it that I love."

"It's gorgeous." Gretchen moved closer to the painting to admire it. The blues and greens seemed to jump off the canvas. "Now I see why you were checking out the light in the upstairs bedroom so intensely."

"Guilty as charged," Charlotte said. "I intend to make the

room that faces the ocean my studio. Don't worry, I'll put something down on the floors to keep the paint off of them."

Gretchen smiled. "I'm looking forward to seeing some of your other works."

"Knock, knock," a man said as he pushed the front door open. "Char, I've got the rest of your stuff in my car."

"It's my brother," Charlotte explained. "Come in!" she called before Gretchen could beat a hasty retreat.

Parker walked in and his eyes met Gretchen's. "Hi," he said. "Long time no see."

She stared at him then turned to walk toward the kitchen and the door to the backyard. Was he seriously acting like everything was okay between them?

He caught up with her and tugged at her shoulder to get her to turn around. Her shoulder burned where his fingers brushed against her thin silk blouse. She stopped, unsure of what she was feeling. Part of her wanted to give him another chance, but was there even hope for the two of them?

"Gretchen, wait." He dropped his hand. "I'm sorry about earlier. I didn't mean what I said. Well, giving a new client a bottle of Scotch to seal the deal is a pretty common practice at our company, but I didn't mean to imply that I didn't care about you."

She said nothing.

"I know we haven't known each other long, but I have grown to care for you. If I didn't need this job, I would have given it up immediately." His shoulders slumped and he twisted his fingers. "Can you forgive me?"

Charlotte approached them. "What's going on here? I feel like I'm missing something." She punched him lightly on the arm.

Parker turned to his sister. "I was a jerk earlier and I'm begging Gretchen for forgiveness."

"Over a rental application?" Charlotte's eyes flitted between the two of them. "I'm so confused. How do you two know each other?"

"We've known each other for a little over a week," he said tersely.

"Wait, before we saw the house?" But her question fell on deaf ears.

"Gretchen, can you just think about forgiving me?" He reached out to touch her again.

Tears welled in her eyes and she moved out of his reach. "I don't think so."

Her heart pounded. She wanted to forgive him, but after all of this, how could she trust him? This job was so important to her and he acted like she was someone for him to steamroll in a business transaction.

"You don't understand," he said. "Let me explain."

"No, I do understand." She turned the back doorknob. The carriage house and freedom seemed so close, yet so far away. "I don't want to hear your explanations." With trembling hands, she pulled the door open and stepped out onto the back porch. After reaching the safety of the carriage house, she glanced back. Parker stood in the doorway, staring wordlessly at her.

Parker watched Gretchen's retreating form until she entered the carriage house. A minute later, old-school pop music blared out of her apartment—probably to discourage him from coming any closer. He shook his head. She wasn't making this easy.

"Do you mind telling me what's going on?" Charlotte asked, coming up behind him.

"It's complicated."

"I've got time." She grabbed his hand and dragged him into the living room, then pushed him toward the couch. "You don't look good, big brother," she observed. "Do you want something to drink? I think I know where I packed the mugs and the coffeepot. Although, now that I think about it, I'm not sure where the coffee is."

Parker grinned. His little sister's organizational abilities were hit or miss. "A glass of water would be great."

She squeezed his shoulder. "Coming right up."

When she was out of the room, Parker gazed longingly at the front door. He really didn't want to get into this with his sister, but if he cut out of there, he'd never hear the end of it from her or his mother.

"Here you go." Charlotte pushed a glass of water at him.

"Thanks." He sipped some water and then rolled the cool glass between his hands.

"So tell me about what's going on with you and my landlord." She perched on the edge of the coffee table and faced him.

"We met at the chocolate festival the weekend before last," Parker said. "We sampled some chocolates together and then I invited her to lunch at the Bluebonnet Café." He stared up at the ceiling. "I feel weird talking to you about this."

"You used to tell me everything."

"Yeah, back when that meant telling you I got a 'D' on a math test."

"So you liked her..." Charlotte prodded.

"Yes. I liked her. Still like her," he corrected himself. "The problem is, she's the daughter of the owners of Candle Beach Real Estate."

"Ooh. That is bad. But you're an adult. Are you really telling me that you two are fighting over Mom and Dad's silly feud with her parents?"

"No. That was bad, but what's worse is that she and I are now competing for the same job—the sales role at the new development south of here, just off the highway."

"Oh, I've seen the signs for it. The houses look like they'll be beautiful. Nice views of the water and big lots." Her gaze turned dreamy. "Maybe if the shop is a success I'll be able to afford one of them." She grinned at Parker. "In my fantasies at least."

He mock-glared at her. "I thought we were talking about me, here."

She waved her hands in the air. "Okay, sorry. So what are you going to do? Let her have the job?"

"I can't." He leaned against the back of the couch. "This development and job are my chance to break out on my own."

"No Gray and Associates for you?" she teased. "I thought I was the only one still living here that they were going to let out of the family business." She paused and became serious. "Are things really getting that bad with Graham? I know our big brother is a stick-in-the-mud and you two have never gotten along, but I thought you'd patched things up."

"No, it's gotten worse. He doesn't respect me, no matter how much business I bring in." He sighed. "I'm branching out on my own whether or not I get this job. The commissions for this would help with startup expenses. But..." He trailed off.

"But if you take the job, Gretchen will never speak to you again and you lose the girl," she finished. "I see your conundrum."

"Yeah, that and I said some things to her about the job that may not have been the most considerate." He sighed again. "So as a woman, do you see any way possible that she'd forgive me?" He hoped his sister could come up with a solution, because he certainly didn't see one—at least not a good one.

"Based on the way she stormed out of here after seeing you, you have a very slim chance of getting her back. The only way you might make it work is to give in and concede the job to her."

"I don't know if I can do that." He ran his fingers through his hair. This situation kept getting messier and messier.

"Well, if you want her back, it's the only way." The dreamy expression filled her eyes again. "I mean, doesn't it seem like fate that you bumped into her at the chocolate festival, then she turns out to be my landlord, and you're both real estate agents? Big brother, the world is throwing you together."

"Fate?" he echoed. "Maybe." He pushed himself up from the couch. "Let's get my car unloaded before it starts to rain again."

"Sure." She opened the front door, then pivoted in the doorway to address him. "But think about what I said. If you don't take this opportunity, you may not get another chance."

He nodded and followed her to the car. If nothing else, at least he'd still have opportunities to see Gretchen since Charlotte now lived across the lawn from her. Even if the job situation didn't end well, he may be able to convince her to give him another chance.

∾

The phone rang early on Friday morning before Gretchen left for work. She put down the frying pan she'd been washing and dried her hands on a dish towel. Soap bubbles scented with Dawn dish detergent floated in clusters in the sink, catching the sunlight. She picked up the phone, afraid to find out who was calling.

"Ms. Roberts?" Martin's deep voice asked.

She almost dropped the phone in the mound of soap bubbles.

"Yes?" Her heart pounded. If he told her that her plea to be considered for the job hadn't worked, she didn't know what she'd do.

He didn't mince any words.

"I'd like you to come work for me."

"Really? You mean it?" She covered the phone and squealed at Reilly before returning to the call. "I mean, that's great. Thank you."

Exhilaration shot through her, electrifying her nerves and numbing her legs. She leaned against the kitchen counter. The extra time she'd put into her presentation had paid off. She'd won the job and beaten Parker. Then she sobered. If this job hadn't come between Parker and herself, would their relationship have worked? She shook her head. There wasn't any point in dwelling on what could have been.

"There's more though." He cleared his throat.

"More?" There were more hoops for her to jump through?

"I've decided to hire both you and the other candidate," he announced.

"I'm sorry, I don't think I heard you correctly. You're going to hire both of us?"

"Yes. My original decision to hire the other person still stands, but you impressed me with your initiative and drive. I think you and Parker Gray will make a great team."

"A great team..." she echoed. Jumping through hoops sounded more appealing than working with Parker.

"Yes. Do you know Parker?"

"We've met." Her voice stretched thinly across the words. Should she tell him right now that she didn't want to work with Parker? Her stomach had turned into knots and she couldn't get the words out. "Are you sure you want to hire both of us? Won't it make things more complicated? I know I can handle everything on my own."

"I don't doubt that you can, but I think having two agents will make things easier. Are you saying you don't want to work on a team?"

"No, no." She almost tripped over her words in her haste to get them out. "That's not what I mean. I'm sure Parker and I will work well together."

"Great. How about if we all meet on Tuesday morning to discuss how this will work? Say at ten o'clock?"

"Ten o'clock it is. I'm looking forward to meeting with you again...and Parker of course. Thank you." She hung up and plunked down on one of the kitchen chairs. Reilly sensed something was off and trotted over to her. He put his head in her lap. Petting his ears usually soothed her, but today her mind kept spinning.

What had just happened? Martin had given her the job, but she wouldn't have full sales responsibilities and she'd have to share the commissions with Parker. Honestly, part of her was relieved that she wouldn't be fully responsible for all of the sales operations. She knew she could handle it if necessary, but it would be nice to have someone there with more extensive sales experience.

But why did it have to be Parker Gray? Now there would be no avoiding him. She'd have to see him every day at work. Could she handle that? Was the job worth the added stress?

12

"*I*'m not going to take the job." Gretchen stared at the raspberry-filled donut on her plate. It had sounded good when she ordered it, but now she had no appetite. The grease- and sugar-scented air combined with her anxiety made her feel nauseous. She shifted positions and the metal chair scraped against the scarred tile floor.

"What are you talking about?" Eliza Roberts put down her mocha and peered into her daughter's eyes. Gretchen had called her that morning and asked to meet her at Donut Daze for an afternoon break.

"I wanted the job to be independent and show that I can excel at sales. Now I have to share the position with someone else. It's just not worth it."

"And that's all you're upset about?" Eliza asked. "This wouldn't have anything to do with the person you're sharing the position with?"

As usual, her question was on point. Gretchen squirmed under her mother's scrutiny. "Okay, so maybe a little of it has to do with Parker." She pushed the donut around on her plate, making patterns in the powdered sugar. "I don't want to have to see him every day."

"So you still have feelings for him?" Eliza asked. She scanned Gretchen's face.

"I barely know him." Gretchen looked away. Outside, raindrops sprinkled onto the pavement and the sky had taken on a gray tinge. Donut Daze was almost empty at two o'clock in the afternoon, but she knew that would change in a few weeks when the tourists started to arrive for the summer season. Then, the room would be filled with the clanging of the espresso machine and the chatter of patrons crowded around the royal blue, too-small tables.

"But you have feelings for him," Eliza stated again.

"Yes. No. I don't know." She gazed at the ceiling. "Argh! Why does this all have to be so complicated? I wish I'd never met Parker Gray."

"Sorry, that's the way life works. To be honest, I wish we'd never entered into that business deal with his parents. Maintaining a feud for this long in a small community has been exhausting."

"So what really happened between you guys?" Gretchen was happy to have anything to take her mind and her mother's attention off of her current predicament. She leaned back in her chair.

Eliza shrugged. "The local population was exploding twenty years ago and we decided to go in with the Grays on ownership of a small apartment building in Haven Shores. We'd met them at a real estate conference and they seemed like great people."

Gretchen looked at her with interest. "So what happened?"

"We had a run of bad luck. Plumbing leaks, roof repairs, etc. The building became costly. We disagreed on how to manage it." Her gaze went blank as she recalled the details. "Things fell apart from there. There wasn't really one thing I can point to that broke the camel's back. It was a combination of all of those things. Anyways, we sold the building at a loss and we never spoke to them again. Each couple blamed the other for the failed venture."

"So they were never dishonest?" Gretchen asked slowly. "All this time it seemed like something horrible had happened."

"No, they were never blatantly dishonest," she admitted. "Things disintegrated between us, but in truth, it was just an all-around bad business decision."

Gretchen didn't say anything. If Parker's family wasn't to blame for the loss on the apartment building, it created doubts about whether or not he'd known she was up for the same job as him. She'd convinced herself that he came from a family that thought nothing about stomping on other people's feelings, but now she wasn't sure what to believe.

"Now," Eliza said. "Instead of a trip down memory lane, can we concentrate on the issue at hand?"

"There's no issue. The best way to get out of this situation is for me to find another way to earn enough money to move away from Candle Beach."

Her mother frowned, but Gretchen had made up her mind.

Unfortunately, money hadn't miraculously materialized in Gretchen's bank account. After finishing work at Candle Beach Real Estate, she went home and pored over her finances. There was no way she could afford to move to Seattle—not if she wanted to avoid a fiery plummet to the depths of bankruptcy. Renting the house out would bring in enough funds for a small startup account by fall, but she'd still have to find a job in Seattle while she worked on getting situated as a real estate agent.

She needed to find a new job if she wouldn't be earning commissions from the new housing development. She rested her chin on her hands. There had to be some way to make this work. Her eyes fell on the application she'd picked up from Candle Beach Kids. Perfect! In the excitement over the real estate sales position, she'd never completed it. She filled it out and walked into town to give it to Abby.

Abby was busy with customers, but when she finished, she approached Gretchen with a big smile. "Hey, I didn't expect to see you back here."

Gretchen held her application out. "I have my employment references listed at the bottom. I hope the job is still available. I'd love to work here."

Abby's smile slipped. "Oh Gretchen, I'm so sorry. I filled the position last week. I told you I needed your application back by last Wednesday."

She pasted a smile on her face. "I totally understand. If something comes up, please let me know." She turned and exited the store.

Outside, she slid down on a bench and surveyed Main Street. Ordinarily, the colorful flower arrangements next to the building would have cheered her up, but not this time. Main Street was full of businesses, but like Candle Beach Kids, most would already have hired their seasonal help. Was she out of luck?

She'd really screwed this up. She'd put all her eggs in one basket with the sales job and now it looked like there wasn't a way to get out of Candle Beach. Still, there was no way she was going to work with Parker. She'd find another job.

Parker sat on the leather couch in his Haven Shores apartment, staring out at the city street below. The wind blew rain diagonally into the window pane. He watched as the beads of water dissolved upon impact, sliding down the glass. Cars streamed past the building as workers navigated the evening rush hour. A police siren sounded in the distance, but he barely heard it. His uneaten sub sandwich rested on the glass coffee table.

Had it really only been a week ago that he'd stared into Gretchen's eyes at Arturo's and been hit by the realization that she could be the one? He'd spent his twenties dating women who couldn't put more than a few words together in a sentence. That wasn't cutting it anymore. Gretchen was confident, funny and smart. Exactly what he'd hoped for in a woman.

Somehow, he'd managed to ruin their relationship almost before it began. Well, she'd had some role in it, but he'd bungled most of their interactions after they found out they were interested in the same job. His mother's interference hadn't helped.

He got up and paced the hallway. A quick glance in the bathroom mirror revealed bloodshot eyes. He hadn't slept more than a few hours at a time since his interview for the sales position.

Gretchen had been devastated when she saw him in the parking lot outside the sales office on the day of her first interview. Then, he'd made it worse when he returned with the marketing materials and caught her coming out of her second interview. It was all such a mess.

He had briefly considered turning down the job when Martin offered it to him. But he couldn't do that. Not if he wanted to get out on his own and not be trading on the family name and business for the rest of his career. If he stayed at Gray and Associates, his older brother's shadow would always hang over him. This position could be the catalyst for a successful future in real estate.

Now that Martin wanted to hire both of them for the job, maybe he had a chance with Gretchen. His spirits lifted. She may think she hated him, but he'd keep trying to win her over. She would eventually understand that he needed this job as much as she did, right? He hoped he could wear her down.

"You're really going to give up so easily?" Maggie asked with an incredulous look on her face. She'd come over late Friday afternoon, seemingly only to give Gretchen a hard time about the job. She sat down in one of the two chairs wedged into the carriage house's small kitchen area.

"It wasn't an easy decision." Gretchen sighed. "I don't feel like I have any other choice."

"You always have another choice." Now Maggie wore the disapproving mom face that she used with Alex. Gretchen hated seeing that expression on her friend. With her even temper and calm way of looking at life, Maggie was usually right. "What's the worst that could happen if you take the job?"

"Parker sells circles around me and I look like a fool? Or it becomes too miserable at work being around him?" Her thoughts spiraled downward and she wasn't convinced she'd made the right decision.

"Have you told Martin yet that you plan to decline the job offer?"

She scooted her chair back and stared at the ceiling. "No. I figured I'd wait until Monday."

"Something's holding you back," Maggie observed. "Otherwise you would have called him immediately after you made the decision."

"No, nothing's holding me back. However, that doesn't mean I'm looking forward to the conversation." She'd spent so much time convincing Martin to hire her that she felt foolish declining his offer. But sharing the position with Parker had never been her intention. This was a completely different situation than she'd signed on for. She hadn't even accepted the offer and she already felt drained.

"Because you know it would be in your best interest to take the job." Maggie swept her hands in the air. "Look around. You're living in a carriage house instead of the house you love."

"Yeah, so? What does that have to do with the sales job?"

"You're willing to give up your house and live in this tiny space because it gets you closer to your goal of moving to Seattle, but you won't do the one thing that has the possibility of making that dream a reality." Maggie sighed. "I don't understand what's going through your head."

"I can figure out a way to achieve my goal without taking the job with Parker."

"Yeah, you can work a part-time job for minimum wage." Maggie stood and paced in circles along the length of the loveseat. "Do you know how long it will take you to earn enough money at the rate you're going? Probably years."

From the double bed on the other side of the room, Reilly's eyes followed Maggie's pacing. His ears perked up as if he was listening to his owner and her friend argue.

"I'll make it work," Gretchen said stubbornly. Maggie's advice had created doubts in her mind. Would her plan succeed? There had to be a way to make it work without this job.

"If this was truly your dream, you'd do anything you could to make it happen." Her eyes clouded in memory. "I missed years of Alex's life working extra shifts at the café to gain experience before buying out the owner when he retired. I knew it was something I had to do if I wanted to make a real life for us in Candle Beach."

"That was different. You had a son to worry about. I can figure something else out." Gretchen got up and filled a glass with water, and drank deeply. She shivered from the cold water, but felt more alert.

Maggie switched tactics. "Why don't you want to take the job? Is it only because of Parker?"

"Yes, but that's a big only." She drained the rest of the water in one long gulp and refilled it.

"So you're going to let him waltz into your life, create havoc with your emotions and then take your dream job?" Maggie sat on the loveseat and clasped her hands in her lap.

"What's done is done." Gretchen glanced at the clock on the wall. "I'd probably better get going. I promised my parents I'd meet them for dinner."

"It's four o'clock," Maggie said dryly. "Your parents are older, but they're not old enough for the early bird special, and neither are you." She crossed the room to Gretchen. "You're not getting out of this so easily." She stared out the window toward the big house. "Charlotte is Parker's sister, right?"

"Yes, why?" Where was Maggie going with this?

"Well, he's going to be visiting her right across the lawn from you." She pointed to the back door. "You're going to see him, whether you like it or not."

The thought had occurred to Gretchen, but she'd tried to convince herself that Parker wouldn't be around much. But if he had been there to help Charlotte make the rental decision and then to help her move in, they probably had a close relationship. Close enough that he'd be present frequently and she'd have the chance of running into him.

"You can't avoid him," Maggie said. "You might as well take the job and earn some money and experience." She put her hand on Gretchen's arm. "This is your town. You know everything going on here. You deserve this job. Don't let your fear of seeing Parker take that away from you." Then she put her jacket on. "I'll let you get to your 'dinner' plans, but please think about what I said."

The wind slammed the door shut behind her, leaving Gretchen alone. The small space seemed to close in on her. She opened the kitchen window to allow fresh air to fill the room. The salt-scented air reminded her of the view she'd given up by renting out the main house. It hadn't been very long and she already missed seeing the ocean first thing in the morning when she woke up.

She looked across the lawn at Gram's house. Maggie was right that she couldn't avoid Parker. But did it make sense to take the job and have to see him every day? As much as she wanted to not feel that way, every time she saw Parker it was like a sharp piece of glass cut into her soul. How had that man gotten under her skin so quickly? And how could she make the feeling stop?

~

Gretchen collapsed on the bed and hugged Reilly. "Am I doing the right thing?" He licked her hand. She lay next to him, enjoying his warmth. Sometimes it was nice to have someone to love you unconditionally.

She scanned the room. Maggie was right; the carriage house was small for one person, but downright tiny when you added in a medium-sized dog. She'd sacrificed their roomy house to get closer to her goal. How could she give up on something that would get her even closer to that goal?

"Reilly, let's go." She grabbed her coat and his leash off the hooks by the door. He raced to the door. She clipped the leash on his collar and they walked out through the gardens to the main street.

A walk usually cleared her mind. She hoped it would work its magic this time. They trotted at a brisk pace down the hill toward town and the beach access trail.

The tourists hadn't arrived yet and the beach was practically deserted. Candle Beach had a strict on-leash policy, so she let out Reilly's leash to give him the maximum length to run. Seagulls gathered at the shoreline, wading in the surf and squawking amongst them. Reilly tried unsuccessfully to reach them while leashed, but only succeeded in scattering a few.

The sun had fallen low in the sky and the temperature had dropped. She shivered and zipped up her jacket. Reilly pranced on the sand and she laughed at his antics. She couldn't wait until summer came and she could take him to the beach more often without drowning in the rain.

Candle Beach, both the town and the beach itself, were breathtaking in the summer. She thought back to last summer's Founder's Day festival and how cute Maggie's little boy had been in the parade. The whole town had come out to celebrate and Gretchen had ridden on a parade float herself. Labor Day weekend had been crazy with all the tourists, but there was something wonderful about seeing the whole town come together, townies and tourists alike.

Would she be able to find that sense of community in a bigger city? Would she have friends with whom to celebrate the good times and the bad? She could always come back to Candle Beach to visit, but it wouldn't be the same. Maggie and Dahlia would move on with their lives and there would always be in-jokes and things that she was no longer a part of.

She sighed. Time to start walking again. Being alone with her thoughts wasn't working so well.

She whistled for Reilly and tugged at his leash. He jogged over to her and stayed by her side as they climbed up the beach access stairs to Main Street. In front of Pete's Pizzeria, a crowd of friends had gathered. They stood in a circle, chatting. One person must have told a funny story, because his friends all laughed in unison.

A twinge of pain shot through her. She'd miss the town and her family, but most of all, she'd miss her friends. In the past year, she'd bonded with Maggie and Dahlia and it felt like together, they could handle anything. Now, if she left town, she'd break that connection.

She turned away from the pizzeria and started up the hill toward her house.

A woman was jogging down the hill. She wore patterned yoga pants and a turquoise tank top, not seeming to notice the cold. She stopped in front of Gretchen and jogged in place as she pulled ear buds out of her ears. Reilly recognized her and nudged against her leg.

"Hey." She lowered herself to pet Reilly, who rubbed his head against her hand. "I thought that was you."

"Charlotte, hi," Gretchen said. "I didn't know you were a

runner." In reality, other than her excellent credit score, she didn't know much about her tenant.

Charlotte laughed. "Oh, I'm not. It seemed like a good idea. New town, fresh start. I'm trying to convince myself I love exercising."

Gretchen smirked. "I know what you mean. Every few months, I try to convince myself of the same thing."

"We should 'exercise' together sometime." She wiggled her eyebrows at Gretchen. "How does a downhill run and then a stop at the donut shop sound? We could walk back."

"Sounds like my kind of exercise." Gretchen stopped. What was she doing? Making friends with Parker's sister had trouble written all over it.

"Oh, I meant to congratulate you on the new job. Parker told me you were both chosen to sell the properties at that new housing development." Charlotte pushed herself up from her crouched position. "That's so exciting."

"It is, thank you," she said automatically. This was why making friends with Parker's sister wouldn't work. Her brain was going crazy. What was she supposed to say to her about the job? Should she admit that she wasn't going to take it? Did she even want to do that?

"I bet you two will be working closely together," Charlotte said slyly.

"Not too closely. We'll both be trying to sell the properties on our own."

"Of course. But you'll see each other every day, that's all I meant." Charlotte smiled. "It's great that two locals were chosen for the sales job. Between the two of you, you must know everything going on in this part of the coast."

Gretchen nodded, but anxiety had crept in. Charlotte's words echoed Maggie's sentiment. With her knowledge of the coastal area, she would have the ability to provide good service to potential clients. But it came with the price of working with Parker.

Charlotte seemed to notice her distress and changed the subject.

"I'm so excited to be opening Whimsical Delights next week." She danced in place. "This has been my dream for so long. All those years of working at my parent's business to save up for it." Her face glowed with pride.

"I'm happy for you," Gretchen said. "Do you plan to keep it open in the winter, or only operate it in the summer season?" Charlotte's lease went until the end of September, so she wasn't sure of her tenant's plans after that.

"I'm not sure." She shrugged. "I'm hoping it's a raging success and I'll be able to make enough in the summer months to keep it open during the winter. If that doesn't work out, I'll reassess my plans."

"I think that's what a lot of the business owners here do."

"Hey, I never asked, but I'm assuming it's alright for me to keep my excess inventory in the house."

"That's fine," Gretchen replied. "I wondered why you wanted such a big house for only one person. I have to admit I was surprised that it was just you."

"Well, that's one reason. The other is that there wasn't much choice in town. But I'm so happy I found your house to rent. It's beautiful."

Gretchen smiled. "Thank you. It belonged to my grand-mother. I have many happy memories there myself." A pang of sadness hit her at the thought of someone else living in Gram's house. But renting it to Charlotte brought her one step closer to her goal of a new life in Seattle. From what she'd observed, she was taking good care of the house. If she had to rent it out, at least she'd found a good tenant.

The sun hung just over the horizon, showering the sky

with vibrant hues of red and pink. She wished she'd brought her camera with her to take a picture of the sunset. That was something she wasn't going to see in Seattle.

The setting sun reminded her of the time. She hadn't lied to Maggie, there really was a family dinner tonight at her parent's house.

"I've got to get to a family thing," she said to Charlotte. "It's been nice talking with you."

"You too," Charlotte said. "And Gretchen?"

"Hmm?"

"Parker really is a good guy. He may not always say or do the right thing, but he has a good heart."

Gretchen nodded and waved at her before tugging on Reilly's leash. She knew Charlotte meant well in her efforts to convince her of Parker's finer qualities, but it wasn't going to work. Her romantic relationship with Parker was over. She needed to decide if she could forge a working relationship with him, or turn down the job and cut ties with him permanently.

13

"*A*re you really dating Gretchen Roberts?" Denise Gray's voice rang out from the speaker of Parker's phone.

He groaned and made a U-turn back into the McDonald's parking lot. How had his mother found out?

"We've been out on a few dates." He unbuckled his seatbelt and grabbed a greasy fry from the bag of takeout on the passenger seat. This could be a lengthy conversation. He might as well eat the fries before they got cold.

"Why didn't you say something to me when I mentioned meeting her in Haven Shores?" Denise accused.

"Because you were already bashing her. She's a nice woman and neither of us needed you butting into our relationship." *They were doing badly enough on their own*, he thought.

"But a Roberts? You couldn't have found someone else? What about your brother's friend? Anastasia?"

"You mean Annabelle." He sighed. "Mom, I have no interest in Annabelle. I need to be focused on my career. I never intended to get involved with Gretchen, it just happened."

"How does something like this 'just happen'?"

He could hear her pacing the floor, like she always did on the phone. His mother had so much nervous energy that she easily maintained a rail-thin figure without exercise.

"We met, we went out on a date. That's how it happened. Not that it's any of your business." He paused. "How did you find out?"

"Charlotte told me."

"Charlotte told you," he repeated. That figured. His younger sister couldn't keep a secret if her life depended on it.

"Yes. She let it slip when she was telling me about your new job. Congratulations, by the way. It's a pity that you have to work with that woman though." She cleared her throat. "I don't know why you didn't tell me yourself about the job."

He tried to calm himself, but anger still seeped through as he spoke. "Mother, please don't talk about Gretchen that way. She's not like her parents. Correction, I don't even know what her parents are like, but if they're anything like her, you and Dad have been holding a nonsensical grudge for way too long."

"Well, it doesn't really matter. Charlotte said you two were on the outs. Probably for the best."

He gritted his teeth. "Charlotte doesn't know what she's talking about. Things are fine between Gretchen and me." That was a total lie, but he wasn't going to give his mother the satisfaction of knowing their relationship was shaky.

"How does she feel about you applying for the job after I told you about it?"

"You shouldn't have said anything to me, Mother. She trusted you."

"Well, you got the job didn't you? I'm proud of you. Sometimes in business, you have to go for things, even if other people get hurt."

"I can't talk to you right now." He hung up the call and stared at the darkened screen. He hadn't sought out Martin after his mother told him about her conversation with Gretchen. He'd told Gretchen the truth. He'd run into Martin the week before meeting her and he had encouraged him to apply for the position at his new development.

When his mother came to his condo to tell him about the job, he hadn't felt any obligation to tell her he already had an interview scheduled. He hadn't wanted to hurt Gretchen by telling her about the call from his mother, but he wasn't sure she'd see it the same way. There was no way she could ever find out about his mother's interference or he'd lose her forever.

∼

"I'm so happy to have my team together." Martin beamed. Gretchen and Parker exchanged awkward glances.

She shifted her weight from foot to foot and leaned against the wall before looking up at Martin. "I'm excited to be here," she said. In truth, she'd rather be at the dentist's office having a tooth pulled, but it didn't seem smart to say that to her new boss.

"We're going to be a great team," Parker said smoothly. "Right, Gretchen?"

She forced a smile and nodded.

"Fantastic." Martin motioned for them to follow him inside. "Here's a map of the development. You can see there are some properties up on the hill here, some further below, the area around the model home, and then a choice few right on the cliff."

"How many houses total?" Parker asked as he scanned the map.

She leaned in to see the map more clearly. "I love how every house has a view of the ocean. That will be a great selling point." They were grouped in sections of about ten houses in each neighborhood within the development.

"There are a total of forty houses available. We've found thirty to fifty building lots to be the best range for community cohesiveness and manageability," Martin said. "Let's get out there and I can show you the sites in person." He strode out ahead of them, waving his arms at the future home sites as he went.

The streets had been paved since she was there the week before. Flags atop metal stakes marked the lot lines between properties. The lots were close together, but she remembered seeing on the plans a few communal green spaces and pocket parks scattered amongst the development. It was strange to see a housing development before the houses were built and landscaped.

She veered off the pavement to get a closer look at an oddly shaped corner lot, but stumbled on a loose rock and pitched forward. Before she hit the ground, a strong arm caught her.

"Careful." Parker smiled his familiar smooth smile and her legs felt as steady as a newborn calf's.

"Thank you," she said stiffly. She hated how cocky he was, but most of all she hated how one glance from him could still make her weak in the knees.

"No problem," he said. "I'm here to help."

Martin was halfway up the street that summited the hill

portion of the development. He turned around to look at what was holding them up.

"Is everything okay?"

"Just peachy," she said through gritted teeth. "We were admiring the view from here."

"I certainly was," Parker said under his breath.

"What did you say?" she hissed.

"Nothing," he said innocently. He held out his hand. "We should get up there."

She ignored his proffered hand and quickened her pace until she'd caught up with Martin. From the top of the hill, the scenery was stunning.

"It should be easy to sell these properties," Parker said.

She pivoted to take in the full circle view. To the west, the ocean stretched out below them, seeming to have no end. From where she stood, she could see parts of Candle Beach and the marina below it. Behind them, in the distance, the highway wound through the old-growth forest like a silver snake. The overall effect was breathtaking. Parker's assessment had been correct. These houses would sell like hotcakes.

"I've owned this property for a number of years, but with the economy on the uptick, this seemed like a good time to build," Martin said. "When I was young, my family summered in Candle Beach, so this development has a special place in my heart."

"Well, we'll make sure that it will be a success, right Gretchen?" Parker put his arm around her and gave her shoulder a quick squeeze. She shrugged out of his embrace as soon as Martin turned away. What was going on with Parker? She'd made it clear she wasn't interested in a relationship with him.

Martin finished his tour of the development and led them back into the sales office trailer.

"The model home should be finished in a few months. At that point, we'll move our operation in there and I'll get a photographer out here to take some pictures of the interior. Until then, I'd like for you two to come up with some sales ideas. We have sketched mock-ups of the exterior of each floor plan, but we need something with more pizzazz. I know I can count on you for that." He smiled at them.

"Of course," she murmured. What could they do that would qualify as pizzazz? Her usual repertoire of sandwich board signs and balloons wasn't going to cut it in this league.

"We'll come up with something perfect," Parker assured Martin.

"I need to get to a meeting in Haven Shores, but I trust you two will be fine here?" He handed each of them a key to the sales office trailer. "Please lock up when you leave." He got into his car and drove out of the parking lot.

Gretchen and Parker stood on the porch of the sales office trailer. The silence was deafening.

"Well," he said. "Let's get started." He motioned to the door. Gretchen trudged into the room and took a seat on one side of the long desk.

"What can we come up with?" He held a ballpoint pen poised over a yellow notepad. "Maybe we should order a pizza? This could take a while."

"I'm fine," she said, although her stomach grumbled. It was past lunchtime and pizza sounded delicious. "I'm here to work, not socialize." She gave him a pointed look. The faster they came up with some ideas, the quicker she could get away from him.

"Okay, okay." He waved his hands up in surrender, but his grin told her he wasn't giving up.

This was going to be a long afternoon. And an even longer time until Oceanview Estates was sold out.

~

May

"I can't believe they got this house up in two months," Gretchen said. She and Parker were inspecting the perimeter of the model home, the first house built in the development.

"I know. Once they poured the foundation and the rain stopped, things went quickly." He touched the rock trim on the outside of the house. "The craftsmanship is great. I've seen some of these developments where they put them up fast and the lack of quality shows. Martin hasn't cut any corners with this construction."

"That will help as we try to sell them." Her nerves rose up again. They'd been working on a marketing plan for the last two months, but now that the model was ready, things were happening fast. They'd scheduled the grand opening celebration for Memorial Day weekend. Thank goodness the construction crew had finished the first home with a week to spare. Even the landscaping had been installed.

"I love what they did with the inlaid stone walkway and the native ferns and shrubs." She admired the overall effect of the house and greenery. All of the floor plans offered a Pacific Northwest architectural style, with exposed cedar beams and natural river stone throughout the houses. Bees flitted among the flowers and birds tweeted as they flew between newly planted trees.

They entered the house. Although they'd watched the frame go up, neither of them had been allowed inside before. It was worth the wait. The interior gleamed and the wide picture windows highlighted the ocean view. A vase of freshly cut roses perched on the dining room table, scenting the room.

Martin walked in behind them. "Nice isn't it?" He glowed with pride.

"It's gorgeous," she said truthfully. She was thankful she'd accepted the opportunity to sell the new houses. She'd had her doubts about working with Parker, but things had leveled out between them to a relationship that wasn't quite friendly, but was courteous and businesslike. In the beginning, he'd tried to rekindle their romantic relationship, but she'd held firm on her decision to work towards her goal of gaining work experience to move to Seattle. She didn't need anything holding her back in Candle Beach.

"Once the whole development is in, this will be the pride of the coast." Martin ran his hand over the glossy granite countertop. "I've decided I'm going to be the first homeowner here."

"You're buying one of these houses?" she asked.

"Yes, that lot a few streets over." Martin pointed through the window at a lot atop the hill. "I spent quite a bit of time in Candle Beach as a child and this seems like the perfect place to build a retirement home for myself and my wife."

Parker nodded. "I wouldn't mind a place here myself. But with it just being me, I'd rattle around in such a big house." He looked over at Gretchen and she averted her eyes.

"Well, I'll leave you to it," Martin said. "I opened the gate and put out the 'Open House' sign, so we could have people come in at any time. Good luck to you both." He walked out the door, shutting it behind him.

She looked around. Two desks had been set up on one side of the open-concept living room. Next to it sat a long table that would be perfect for all of the marketing materials they'd created. "We'd better move our sales materials in here."

"I'll grab the boxes out of the sales trailer." Parker opened the door and propped it open with a large rock before going outside.

He brought in the first set of boxes and set them on the floor. While he returned to the sales office for the rest of the materials, she grabbed a box and unpacked it. She chose the desk closest to the window for her own and sat behind it in the ergonomic desk chair. She ran her fingers over the dark wood desk, marveling at the unmarred smoothness of the surface, then swiveled around in the chair. Everywhere she turned, the beauty of the new house amazed her. How had she gotten so lucky to get this job?

"I see you've made yourself comfortable," Parker observed, coming back in.

She popped up from the chair. "Sorry, I thought I'd get things set up." She looked at her watch. Almost nine a.m. "Martin's right, we could get potential buyers in here anytime with that ad we put in the Haven Shores and Candle Beach newspapers."

As if on cue, a silver sedan pulled into the parking lot. A portly man in his sixties and a svelte woman in a tracksuit got out of the car.

Parker and Gretchen stared at each other. They both started towards the door and became wedged in the door frame as they exited together. His hand rested on the small of her back as he guided her out the door.

Tingling sensations radiated from everywhere his fingers made contact. She hadn't been this close to Parker in a long time. She jumped sideways.

He held his hands up and edged away. "Sorry."

"We've got to work on our exit strategy," she joked, to ease the tension.

The couple was almost to the doorway.

"Hello." She stretched out her hand. "I'm Gretchen."

"And I'm Parker." He stretched his hand out as well. The man and woman looked at them awkwardly, torn between the two.

Gretchen took action and firmly shook the man's hand. Parker followed suit with the woman. The couple introduced themselves as being newly retired residents of Tacoma, a city an hour south of Seattle. They were looking for a summer retirement home as they were snowbirds who wintered in Arizona.

"You're going to love these homes." Gretchen motioned for them to follow her over to her desk in the house. "We have some fantastic floor plans."

The woman started to sit on the other side of her desk, but Parker called out to the couple from the kitchen.

"Would you like to see the house first? Then you'll have a better idea of what you're looking for in a floor plan." He flashed a beguiling smile. The man moved toward him. The woman looked between Parker and Gretchen, unsure of where to go.

Gretchen gritted her teeth. "Or maybe they'd like to see the floor plans first and then take a look at how this house is laid out."

"I really think it's better for them to see the amazing views first," Parker said. He turned to the couple. "Come this way, and I'll show you the first-floor master bedroom and five-piece master bath."

The woman smiled. "We're looking for a first-floor master. I'd love to see it." They walked away from the desks.

Gretchen narrowed her eyes at Parker's retreating form. Parker 1, Gretchen 0. They'd had their first customer and already were experiencing animosity. This was not going to be fun.

14

The weatherman had forecast sun for the Saturday of Memorial Day weekend, but Gretchen hadn't counted on it. For once, the forecast was correct. By eight a.m., the colorful flower thermometer planted in the garden at the model home read 72 degrees.

Since their soft opening last week, things had been rocky between her and Parker. After the disastrous first experience, they'd realized that only one of them could approach each new customer. They'd reached an uneasy truce, but with the stress of a huge influx of potential buyers on Memorial Day weekend, she wasn't sure how long it would last.

She straightened stacks of brochures and floor plans inside the model home while he supervised the catering team outside. He came inside to update her.

"I had them put the food tent over by the Cliffside lots, rather than next to the house. I think it will entice people over to take a look at the premium lots."

Gretchen grimaced. "I had it located next to the house on the plans for a reason."

"Why? I think it makes more sense to have it further away. Plus, then the whole house doesn't smell like barbecued hot dogs and hamburgers. Win–win." He leaned against the doorframe with his arms crossed across his chest.

"The wind," she said. "On this part of the Washington coast, nothing near the cliffs is safe from the wind gusts coming off the water." Under her breath, she added, "Anyone from this area should know that."

He ignored her side comment and waved off her advice. "It'll be fine. I'll have them use extra stakes to secure it."

"Fine," she said tightly. "Do you need help with anything out there?" She examined the interior of the house with a keen eye. "I think I've got everything taken care of in here."

"I could use some help hanging the banners above the entrance."

She followed him to the sales office and they retrieved the heavy canvas sign they'd ordered with the words *Join us for a FREE Memorial Day weekend BBQ*. A smaller banner read *Experience the joys of living in Oceanview Estates*.

They lugged the signs down the long driveway to the main street.

"How are we getting them up there?" Gretchen eyed the arch of the tall wrought iron gate that would stay retracted during the sales event. It must have been ten feet tall.

"Easy," Parker said. "I'll climb up the rocks on the side." He handed her the banner to hold and climbed halfway up the rock columns. His foot slipped and he caught himself on the gate. "Whoa, these might not have been the best shoes for rock climbing." He glanced ruefully at his wingtip leather loafers.

"You think?" She laughed.

"Hey, I'm serious. I don't think I can get any further up."

The top of the gate was still about three feet above him. "It's getting really slippery."

He climbed down and stared at the arched top.

"Now what?" Her eyes twinkled. How was he going to get the banner up there? "Maybe we could get a step stool from the sales office?"

He shook his head. "There aren't any. I looked this morning."

He eyed her shoes. She hadn't yet changed from her sneakers into the high heels she wore for work.

"What if I gave you a boost and you climbed up there? I could hand you the banner and then we'd do the same for the other side."

She gazed up at the top. She'd never been big on heights, but this was only five feet above her head. She could handle that, right? There wasn't time to get a ladder from home before their scheduled opening time and they needed this sign to attract drivers passing by on the highway.

"Okay," she agreed. "But we're getting a ladder to take it down on Monday night."

"Of course." He held out a hand to her. "Do you need help getting up?"

There was no way she was going to get a boost from him.

"I think I'm okay."

She moved closer to the rock wall. *This is just like the trees you used to climb as a kid*, she told herself. One hand over the other. Without thinking any more about it, she climbed high enough to hook the banner on the metal frame.

He handed it to her and she clipped it onto the gate post with two carabineers attached to metal rings on the banner. She released her grip on the side of the gate and climbed down the rock wall until she could jump to safety. Above them, the banner rippled and twisted in the wind.

"One down, one to go." She repeated the process with the banner on the other side of the gate.

"Looks good," he said.

Still at the top, she leaned back to check it out. He was right. They'd ordered the perfect size and it hung tautly over the gate. It would be impossible for anyone passing by to miss it. She was glad they'd decided on this as their big marketing push to start off sales with a bang.

She was still looking at the sign when she moved her right hand down to grab the rock she'd used to hoist herself to that height. Unfortunately, she forgot she'd moved slightly off to the side to view the sign and her fingers slipped uselessly off the side of the rock. She flailed around desperately seeking a handhold. The movement pushed her off balance and she plunged backwards.

Parker saw her fall as though in slow motion. He held out his arms to catch her and she fell into him, knocking him to the ground. They lay together for a moment while they caught their breath. Gretchen's body felt soft and warm against him. Desire raced through his body with the force of a freight train.

"Are you okay?" he asked.

She rolled onto her side in the dirt and sat up. "I think so." She rotated her wrists, wincing a bit. Then she glared at him. "You could have gotten me killed!"

Guilt twisted in his gut. "Gretch. I'm so sorry."

"No, you should have been prepared. This was your responsibility. Why didn't you have a ladder like a sane person?" She stalked up the hill without looking back at him.

He watched her go. She was right—he should have brought a ladder. But with everything else going on, he'd forgotten. If she'd been hurt, he'd never have forgiven himself. He'd tried to play it cool with her at work, but she didn't seem to have any interest in him. This hadn't helped him win any points. He hung the smaller sign on the side of the rock wall and followed her back up the driveway.

When Gretchen got to the top of the hill, she saw a group of people gathered by one of the ocean lots.

"What's going on?" she asked.

A man wearing the uniform of the catering company pointed to the beach below.

Her eyes followed his finger. The red tent that was supposed to shelter the barbecue grill lay on its side on the beach below. Two of the tent supports were bent into awkward angles.

"What happened?" She counted to ten to calm herself. This was a disaster.

"A big gust of wind came up while we were anchoring it to the ground," one of the men volunteered.

She slapped her hand against her forehead. Parker and his bright ideas.

By then, Parker had reached them. "Where's the tent?" he asked. The catering staff looked at the ground.

She glared at him. "Down there."

His face blanched. "Gretchen, I'm sorry. I thought it would be better over here."

She grabbed his arm, towing him into the empty model

home. "We need to talk."

When they were alone, she turned to him. "I told you to have them set it up next to the house." Her eyes bored holes into his face.

"I know," he said. "I'll figure something out to fix this."

"And you almost got me killed by not having a ladder," she accused him.

A nerve on his forehead pulsed. "You could have helped more with the setup. Why did I get stuck with all the outside setup while you were only in charge of lining up a few brochures inside?"

She stared at him. "You never asked me for help. When I said something to you, you said you had everything under control. I didn't feel like you wanted me to help."

He sighed. "I know." He ran his fingers through his hair. "I thought I did have it under control." He looked miserable and she immediately felt bad about being so harsh on him.

"It's okay. We're still figuring out this partnership." She patted him on the arm. He smiled at her and she withdrew her touch before he got the wrong idea. "I'll go home and get a new tent. My friend has one she uses for the summer market, which doesn't start until June." She grinned. "And I'll bring my telescoping ladder so neither of has to visit the hospital emergency room on Monday."

"Thanks." He wrapped his arms around her in a giant bear hug. Before she realized what she was doing, she laid her head on his chest and melted into his embrace. After the stress of the morning, it felt good to be comforted. Then she pulled away. "I'd better get to Candle Beach to get that tent."

"Okay." He grinned. "I'll have the caterer set up next to the house."

She returned his smile. Maybe they'd make good partners yet.

~

"This has been the most exhausting weekend of my life," Gretchen said. "I'm so glad it's over."

"We sold four houses." Parker shrugged. "I'd say that's an accomplishment."

"But now for the cleanup." The catering crew had left at five when the Memorial Day weekend event ended, but their job was just beginning.

"We've got to get this back in order." That would be an all-night job on its own. They'd shown the model home and reviewed floor plans with potential customers all weekend. Other than basic maintenance, they hadn't put much focus on organizing the model home after each long day. Boxes of brochures were pushed haphazardly against a wall and the garbage bins overflowed with red plastic plates and discarded barbecue items.

The event had been a success, but now they had to pay the price.

"Where should we start?" he asked.

"Let's start outside," she replied. "Then we can come inside toward evening when it gets chilly."

He nodded in agreement. "Sounds like a plan. I'll get the trash bags."

Next to the model home, the caterers had removed their cooking paraphernalia, but the canvas tent she'd borrowed from Dahlia remained, as did several bags of garbage. They hauled all of the garbage down to the curb for Tuesday's trash pickup and folded the tent back into the bag. The wind had blown napkins and paper cups around the development, so they spent the next two hours gathering stray garbage. When they couldn't see anything else to pick up, they returned to the house.

Gretchen collapsed on a patio chair on the back deck. "It's like someone threw a raging house party. But without the fun of it." She rubbed her back.

"No kidding." Parker leaned back in a lounger and put his feet up. "That's why I never was the one who threw the parties in college."

They sat that way for a few minutes, enjoying the water view.

"Hey, I saved us some hot dogs, do you want one?" he asked.

"Sure," she said. "But then we've got to get back to cleaning."

He flashed her a smile, then retrieved two hot dogs from the fridge.

"Do you want yours heated up?" He held the two plates on one arm and grabbed two Pepsi colas out of the refrigerator.

"No." It had been a long day and she just wanted something to eat. They sat down at the umbrella table on the deck. She guzzled her soda, savoring the coolness. They sat together in companionable silence.

She peeked at him from behind her soda can. He was quiet, sipping his Pepsi and staring out at the ocean thoughtfully. After the first mishaps with their sales process, they'd developed a good system and had handled everything well over the weekend. Working with him had turned out to not be so bad.

He set his can down on the table. "You ready to start on the inside?"

"Not really, but let's get it over with," she said.

Together, they straightened the stacks of papers, hid the boxes away in a closet and restocked the floor plans. He wiped down the kitchen counters while she swept the main floor.

It was dark outside when they finished. She felt drained, but at the same time, exhilarated. They'd made it through a big marketing push and sold four homes already. Most of all, working with Parker had been a positive experience.

They turned off the lights and walked out to the front porch. The street lights were on, but the area where they'd parked their cars wasn't lit. He walked her over to her car. She put her hand on the door handle and turned back to him, not wanting the weekend to end.

"Nice night out." He jangled his car keys in one hand while looking up at the moon.

"It is," she agreed. The profile of his face glowed in the moonlight, mesmerizing her.

He turned, as if he knew she was watching him. He looked at her and smiled.

His eyes drew her in like a swirling whirlpool that she couldn't get out of. He put his hand on her shoulder and she instinctively moved toward him. He leaned down, planted a soft kiss on her lips, and then stepped back, as if to judge her reaction. She stood motionless for a moment. What had just happened? She was completely over him, right? So why had it felt so good?

"What was that?" she asked in a breathy voice.

He shrugged. "It seemed like the thing to do. You looked so beautiful standing there."

She stared at him, not knowing what to say or think. They'd worked so hard to get an amicable working relationship in place, and now this. Wordlessly, she got into her car.

He got into his own car and drove away. She watched him leave and then put her head on the steering wheel. What was going on? Did she still have feelings for him?

15

*T*uesday morning came too soon. The sun shone through the kitchen window in the carriage house's studio apartment and burned into Gretchen's eyes. She groaned and rolled over in bed, covering her head with a pillow. Reilly barked at her a few times from his perch on the loveseat.

Groggily, she sat up in bed. She needed to take Reilly out for a morning walk before work. Although she took him to Kyra's Doggy Daycare on days she worked, she liked to get some quality time in with him before dropping him off. She regarded her nighttime attire. She'd left her work polo shirt on when she went to bed. Good enough. She pulled on some jeans and a sweatshirt and plodded over to the door. Reilly trotted eagerly behind her.

After Reilly was taken care of, she was slightly more awake but badly in need of coffee. She made a cup of coffee and a piece of toast and carried them over to the kitchen table. While eating alone, she had way too much time to think about Parker and the kiss they'd shared the night before. Did it mean something to him? She'd been exhausted and her defenses were down, but it had felt surprisingly real.

Her alarm rang to notify her it was time to leave for Oceanview Estates. She'd worked out a deal with her parents to work at Candle Beach Real Estate on her two days off and work five days a week for Martin. Mondays and Tuesdays were Parker's days off, so she'd be alone at the sales office today.

She dropped Reilly off at doggy daycare and arrived at work five minutes late, but there wasn't anyone else in the parking lot. After the rush of prospective clients over Memorial Day weekend, today would seem anticlimactic. She unlocked the door to the model home and sat down at her desk to review some paperwork. She noticed she was out of some of the floor plans, so she wrote a reminder on a sticky note and affixed it to her desk. She needed to find the box where they kept the floor plans, but she wasn't sure where Parker had stored them.

She gazed out the window and the temporary parking lot where he'd kissed her drew her attention, bringing back all the emotions of the night before. Her skin tingled and flushed at the memory and she crossed the kitchen to grab a drink of water from the sink.

The sound of crunching gravel outside pushed away her unprofessional thoughts. She smoothed her skirt, walked to the front door and pasted a big smile on her face.

A woman in her mid-forties had exited her car and was assessing the development with a critical eye.

Gretchen called from the porch, "Can I help you?"

The woman's gaze snapped to her. "Yes, I was just admiring the views from here. I'm living in Haven Shores right now, but I work in Candle Beach, so I drive past this development every day. I'd love to live closer to work."

"Well, I can help you with that." She smiled at the woman and held out her hand. "I'm Gretchen."

"Nice to meet you. I'm Natalie."

"This is a wonderful development," Gretchen said. "You've already noticed the views, which will be visible from every house in the development, but let me show you an example of the interior." She smiled and motioned to the front door of the house.

"That would be great." The woman followed her inside.

Gretchen showed her the different floor plans and the examples of interior finishings. As she ticked off the items on her 'must show' list, she gave herself a silent high five. She was on her game. Maybe this would be sale number five and her first solo sale.

"I'd like to see the lots now." The woman walked over to the back patio for a moment. "Which of the houses will have the least obstructed view?"

"That would be the Cliffside lots or even those at the crest of the hill," Gretchen said. "Which would you like to see first?"

The woman thought for a moment. "I'd like to see the Cliffside lots."

A thrill shot through Gretchen. They were the most expensive of all the lots. If she could sell one of those on her own, the commission would be huge.

As they walked the few blocks to the lots Natalie wanted to see, Gretchen made small talk.

"So what do you do in Candle Beach?" she asked. "I've lived there for most of my life, but I don't think we've met before."

"I'm a lawyer at Franklin and Franklin. The elder Franklin retired last year and they brought me on to help out."

"Ah, that makes sense. I've known the Franklin family for years. How do you like working in Candle Beach? It must be different working in a small town."

"You know, I wasn't sure when I started, but I really enjoy it. I have more time to get to know my clients. Candle Beach is such a cute town and I'd love to live there. Or here, if the house meets my needs. I don't know how I can pass up these views." She stared in appreciation at the ocean below.

When they reached the Cliffside, Natalie went off to explore the lots on her own. Gretchen stood to the side to allow her some privacy. She stared off into the vast expanse of ocean and her mind drifted back to the kiss she'd shared with Parker. Which led her back to thoughts of their romantic date at Arturo's and the Haven Shores boardwalk. Was there a possibility of rekindling things? Or had last night been an accident not to be repeated?

A voice broke into her reverie. "Gretchen."

Natalie stood in front of her, looking quite irritated.

"I'm sorry, did you say something?"

"Yes, I've asked you three times about which floor plans are available for that lot." She pointed at the middle lot in the Cliffside section.

"Sorry, I didn't hear you." Gretchen consulted her notes. "It looks like the Haven and the Pacifica plans are available on that lot. Each of those is over 4,000 square feet."

The woman nodded. "Good, I'd hoped for the Pacifica plan."

"Would you like to take a look at the plan again? I've got it right here." She fumbled in her folder for the floor plan, but wasn't able to find it. "I know I had it here."

Natalie gave her an exasperated look. "Can we go back to the model home and look at it? I'd like to take it home to show my husband."

"Sure, no problem."

They sat down at her desk and Gretchen opened her desk drawer to grab a Pacifica floor plan. The sticky note reading, "restock floor plans" caught her eye. She groaned silently. Thoughts of Parker had distracted her and she'd forgotten to get them.

"I seem to be out of them. If you'll wait here, I can go get some from the back room."

Natalie stood. "I've really got to get to work, I have a client meeting. I'll stop by some other time. Thanks for your help." She rushed out of the sales office.

Gretchen leaned back in her chair. She'd lost a sale that could have potentially been the biggest of her career. And all because she'd been thinking about Parker. The unbidden thought swirled around in her head. She had to keep her eye on the prize, or rather her goal to get out of Candle Beach. Parker was a distraction from that goal. Nausea churned in her stomach at the thought of giving up any possibility of a relationship with him, but she knew it was a necessary sacrifice to reach her goals.

When Gretchen arrived at work on Friday morning, Parker was already there. He jogged up to her in the parking lot as soon as she exited her car.

"Hey, good to see you." He smiled at her, but there was uncertainty in his eyes.

"Good to see you too. How's business?" She circled widely around him, determined not to get too close. "Did you make any big sales?"

"I had a few people say they were coming back this weekend with their spouses. One in particular seemed really interested. I think she said she was a lawyer in Candle Beach."

She closed her eyes for a second and then opened them to make eye contact with him. "Did she say her name was Natalie?"

"Yes, I think so. I have her business card inside." He gave her a quizzical look. "Do you know her?"

"She stopped in here on Tuesday, but had to rush off for a business meeting."

"Oh," Parker said. "She didn't mention meeting you. I spent quite a lot of time with her."

They'd had an unspoken rule that whoever worked with a prospective client first would earn the commission unless otherwise discussed. But was that fair in this situation? If Natalie and her husband came back and bought the most expensive property in the development, which of them should get the commission? She didn't respond to him. If Natalie did return, they could deal with it then.

"So, do you want to talk about it?" he asked.

"About what? That woman?"

"No. About the kiss on Monday night." He brushed his hand through his hair.

"We were both exhausted. It didn't mean anything." She pushed past him to get into the model home. This mess with Natalie reminded her of how dangerous it could be to get involved with him.

He cornered her at her desk. "It didn't feel like nothing."

"Well, it was." She turned on her laptop. "If you don't mind, I've got work to do." It seemed to take forever for the computer to boot up.

He stared at her. "Sure, no problem."

≈

Gretchen raised her face to the late June sun and relished the warmth. It felt good after being stuck inside day after day. Between her two jobs, she hadn't had a day off in over a month and it was starting to wear on her. Dahlia had called her that morning while she was with a client at Candle Beach Real Estate. She'd left a voicemail asking for her to come to the To Be Read booth at the summer market over her lunch break.

The market was in full swing at noon and she had to weave her way between people balancing loads of veggies and flowers to get to the bookstore's booth. A small child engrossed in licking a gigantic ice cream cone bumped into her as he walked past with his mother.

"Sorry!" he cried. His weary mother looked over her basket of fruit and shook her head. "Sorry," she mouthed as they walked away.

Gretchen smiled. If she had an ice cream cone that big in front of her, she wouldn't want to take her eyes off it either.

"Well, I almost got a photo of you covered in ice cream," someone teased her from behind.

She turned. "Adam, hi." He wore a casual t-shirt and khaki shorts, with his camera hanging on a strap around his neck.

"How's it going? I haven't seen you around much."

"I know. I've been really busy with work, both at the new development and in town. It's been a crazy summer."

He nodded. "We should get together sometime and catch up. I'd love to hear about your new job." He grinned at her.

Her mind raced. Was he asking her out on a date again? If so, did she want to go out with him? Dating a guy she wasn't friends with first hadn't worked out so well for her. There was something to be said for knowing someone for a long time. At least with Adam, she knew what she was getting.

"Sure, that would be great. It's been a while since we hung out." She smiled at him. Adam was a nice guy, so why not take a chance on him? After all, she was totally over Parker, right?

"Really? How about Friday? We could grab dinner."

"Sounds good. Maybe around six?"

"Six it is." He smiled at her again.

Then Dahlia waved at her from across the green.

"Oh, I've got to go. I'm meeting Dahlia."

"See you Friday." He waved at her and then wandered off with his camera up to his eye.

Gretchen approached Dahlia's booth.

"Hey, you made it." Dahlia got up and hugged her friend. "I wasn't sure you got the message."

"Yep, and I'm happy to be out of the office. This sun feels great."

"You are looking a little pale," Dahlia said. "You need to get out more."

"I know. And when things settle down, I will. For now, I just have to deal with the long days. More days of work means more money in my bank account."

"I know the feeling." Dahlia motioned for her to sit down.

"So what's this all about?" Gretchen asked.

"Can't I want to see my friend for no reason?"

"Sure, but you sounded like it was important." She leaned back in the chair and smelled the warm air. From off in the distance, seagulls chattered, their voices competing with the crowds at the summer market. In the park, beyond the market, picnickers lay lazily on blankets spread out across the green grass. Summer at the beach couldn't be beat.

"Remember how you wanted me to ask my mother about jobs at her real estate firm?"

Gretchen sat up. "Yeah. What did she say?"

"Well..." Dahlia said, drawing it out.

"What?" Gretchen asked eagerly. "Does she have anything for me?"

"Actually, she does." Dahlia smiled smugly. "She said if you can start in two weeks, there's an opening for an apprentice at her firm."

"Oh my gosh," Gretchen wrapped her arms around her friend. "That's amazing. Thank you, thank you."

"So that's a yes?"

Two weeks. Was that enough time to wrap things up here in Candle Beach? And what about her job at Oceanview Estates? She'd fought so hard for the job and made a commitment to Martin. Could she really give that up? And what about Parker? Things had been strained between them after their kiss on Memorial Day, but a little part of her wondered if maybe someday they would rekindle things. Her elation deflated.

"Yes...no. I don't know. Can I think about it?"

"Sure. But she needs an answer by next week. Here's her number." She pulled out a business card imprinted with her mother's name and contact information and handed it to Gretchen.

Gretchen held up the card, staring at it as though it were made of gold. "I really appreciate this, Dahlia."

"No problem." She looked thoughtful. "If you decide not to take the job, don't feel bad. I of all people know how hard this town is to leave. It really grows on you. And certain people do too." She blushed.

"Thanks. I've got to grab a sandwich before I get back to work, but let's get together sometime soon, okay?"

A customer approached the To Be Read booth. Dahlia nodded to Gretchen and waved goodbye.

Gretchen rubbed her fingers across the smooth cardstock. Like the sales job with Martin, the job offer from Dahlia's mother had the power to change her life. But was leaving town really what she wanted?

Gretchen stared at herself in the mirror. Friday had come all too fast. For her date with Adam, she wore a knee-length skirt and a short-sleeved blouse. Nothing too revealing. Butterflies flitted around in her stomach, but she tried to push them back.

She heard footsteps on the carriage house's exterior stairs. She took another look in the mirror and smiled at her reflection. *You're going to have a good time,* she told herself. *Adam is a great guy.* Reilly sighed from the bed. Even he had his doubts about this date.

Adam really was a nice guy though, and was one of her oldest friends. Although there had never been a romantic spark between them before, it could happen, right? They'd both changed over the years.

She opened the door before he had a chance to knock.

"Hey," he said warmly. "You look beautiful."

She smiled at him and smoothed her skirt. "Thanks. Where are we going tonight?"

They walked down the stairs together.

"I was thinking Arturo's in Haven Shores. They're supposed to have excellent food. Have you heard of it?"

Her heart dropped to her knees and she stopped mid-step, grasping the railing. "I have. I went there a few months ago. The rumors were right, it was great."

It pained her to remember her date there with Parker. Everything had seemed so magical that night and now things between them could be classified as strained at best.

"Do you mind going again? I'd hoped to review it for the newspaper."

"Sure, no problem," she lied. She was over Parker. Maybe eating at the restaurant where they'd had their first date would help her prove it to herself.

"Great." Adam whistled as he walked to his car parked in the alley. He stopped next to the passenger side and opened the door, motioning for her to take a seat.

She released her iron grip on the railing, took a big breath, and hurried down the remaining steps.

"Thanks," she said as she ducked around him to sit. She arranged her skirt around her legs. *Give the guy a chance*, she told herself. She'd dated someone new and look how that had turned out. Maybe dating a friend was exactly what she needed.

He smiled over at her and turned on the radio. "Is this station okay?"

"Yes." She forced brightness into her voice. "So, how's everything going at the paper? It's been a slow news season this year, compared to last summer."

"It has. But there have been new businesses opening in Candle Beach and the surrounding areas. I'm also thinking about writing a feature about Oceanview Estates. Do you think you and your partner would be willing to be interviewed?"

"My partner?" she echoed. Her stomach twisted at the mention of Parker. "Uh, yeah. We'd love the publicity. The development will be beautiful when it sells out. And with forty new houses, it should help the economy around here too."

"Exactly what I was thinking." He smiled at her. "Great minds think alike."

They made polite chit-chat the rest of the way to Haven Shores.

When they arrived at Arturo's, he opened the door for her. They were seated immediately near a window with a wonderful view of the ocean. It should have been romantic, but all she could think about was how much she wanted the date to end. Not because he was bad company, but because he wasn't Parker. Her date with Parker had been special and nothing could compare to it. She tried her best to shrug off the feeling, but conversation between them was stilted during dinner and they were soon on their way home.

He followed her up the stairs to her apartment over the garage. "Well, goodnight," Adam said.

She unlocked the door and pushed it open. "Goodnight." She stepped back into the room in case he had any ideas of a good night kiss.

He smiled at her. "I had a nice time tonight."

"Me too. But Adam—"

He cut her off. "I know. We've been friends for so long, I thought there might be something between us. But you're still hung up on that guy you were dating in the spring, aren't you?"

She smiled at him sadly. "I don't know. I'm sorry. I had a good time with you though."

He gave her a quick hug. "It's okay. Friends?"

She nodded and waved goodbye to him before closing the door. She watched through the window as he trudged down the stairs with his hands in his pockets. She hadn't meant to hurt him, but it didn't seem right to lead him on.

There wasn't a romantic spark between them and their date at Arturo's had made that all too clear.

The next week, Gretchen needed a gift for her cousin, so she visited Charlotte's shop next to Pete's Pizzeria for the first time.

"Hey, you finally came to check out Whimsical Delights." Charlotte bounced off the steps of the Airstream trailer to hug Gretchen, who put down the lawn gnome she'd been admiring outside. "Come in," she said, grabbing her hand and pulling her into the shiny metal vehicle.

"I love your store." Gretchen's eyes adjusted to the dim light as she followed the flower decals on the floor all the way to the back. "I can't believe how much you've packed in here."

"Yeah, my brother says it's too much, but I maintain there can never be too much merchandise in a store." Charlotte looked proudly around her boutique.

"How has business been?"

"It's been great. We got that huge rush of customers last weekend and it paid for my site rent for half a month. If this keeps up, I should be able to keep Whimsical Delights open year round."

"That's great," Gretchen said. "I'm happy for you."

"So what brings you in today? Are you looking for anything in particular?"

"Something for my cousin, Nora. It's her birthday next week. She always gets me something fun and I usually get her a boring gift like a bottle of lotion."

"What does she like?" Charlotte asked. "We have a little of everything here."

"I can see that." She laughed. "She's into frogs. Her kitchen is full of frog-themed items."

Charlotte snapped her fingers. "I've got the perfect thing. I got these on my last buying trip to a craft market in Oregon." She opened a lower cabinet and took out a comical pair of princess and frog salt and pepper shakers.

"Those are so cute." Gretchen examined the pair. "She'll love them." She handed them back to Charlotte, who set the shakers on a piece of butcher paper.

"Oh, and I saw something that made me think of you." She walked over to a rotating rack of magnets. "Here," she said, handing one to Gretchen.

It was a magnet the size of her palm with a boxer dog on it. "It looks just like Reilly," Gretchen said.

"I know! Reilly could have been the model. I think you should have it. It's on the house."

"Thanks," Gretchen said. "I love it." To her surprise, over the last couple of months, Charlotte had become a good friend.

"You're welcome." Charlotte beamed. "I love giving people things."

"Yeah, well, hopefully you don't give all your customers gifts. You won't make a profit like that."

"Only my friends." Charlotte rang up the salt and pepper shakers. "Do you want these in a gift bag?"

"Yes, please." That would save her a step. Gift-giving wasn't Gretchen's forte.

"So how are things going between you and Parker?" Charlotte asked nonchalantly.

"Why do you ask?" She handed Charlotte her credit card.

"No reason. Just wondering." She shrugged. "I thought you'd have made up by now."

How much had Parker told his sister? Did Charlotte know about their kiss on Memorial Day?

"We work together. That's it."

"But it could be more," Charlotte pressed. "He likes you and you like him."

"It's complicated," she said.

"It doesn't have to be." Charlotte gave her a beguiling smile.

"Look, I don't mean to be rude, but it's really not any of your business. Parker and I have a professional relationship and that's how it needs to stay."

Charlotte shrank back and Gretchen sighed. She hadn't meant to offend her, but she was getting a little tired of her prying into her love life, even if it was to promote her brother. "I'm sorry. It's been a rough couple of weeks at work." She eyed the door. The narrow walls of the Airstream were making her feel claustrophobic.

"How so?" Charlotte leaned forward on the tiny counter.

"I don't really want to talk about it."

After the kiss on Memorial Day, Gretchen and Parker had barely spoken. They'd communicated about sales opportunities and that was the sum total of their relationship. That was how it had to be if she wanted to keep him from being a distraction to her success. Sometimes though, he would catch her eye and smile and her resolve would weaken. Was she doing the right thing by shutting him out of her life?

"Okay, but if you ever need an ear, I'm here." Her expression turned serious. "I meant what I said. I consider you a friend and I care about you, even if there isn't a future between you and Parker."

"Thanks." She took the gift bag with the salt and pepper shakers and stepped out of the Airstream. Once outside, she took a deep breath of the warm, salty air. Whimsical Delights was a nice place to visit, but she didn't know how Charlotte managed to be inside the small metal trailer for long periods of time.

Gretchen couldn't put off calling Dahlia's mom any longer. The job in Seattle could be a huge boon for her career, but she wasn't feeling one hundred percent ready to leave Candle Beach. Images of Parker kept entering her mind and muddling her thoughts. She'd assumed by now she'd be over him, but with the constant reminders from her friends of what they could have been, he was hard to forget. Not to mention seeing him almost every day at work.

She picked the business card off her kitchen table and dialed.

"This is Vanessa," Dahlia's mother said in clipped tones.

"Hi, this is Gretchen Roberts, Dahlia's friend in Candle Beach."

"Hi Gretchen, how are you? Are you excited about Dahlia's wedding? I can't believe she's getting married. Her father and I are so happy for her."

"Yes, I'm looking forward to being a bridesmaid." She fingered the sharp edge of the business card. "I was calling about the job in Seattle."

"Of course," Vanessa said smoothly. "Does starting in two weeks sound good to you? We really need to get someone in here ASAP."

"Actually, that's what I wanted to talk to you about." She hesitated. "Do you think there's any way the job might still be open in a few months?"

"In a few months?" Vanessa sounded puzzled.

"Yes, I'm actually working as a sales agent for a housing development here and expect to be finished sometime in the fall. I was hoping the job could be held until then." She crossed her fingers. It was a long shot, but worth a try.

"I'm sorry, we can't do that. It's imperative we have someone start right away. Are you sure you can't take the job? I know you'd be perfect for it and it would be fantastic experience."

Unbidden thoughts of Parker crossed her mind again, along with a feeling of sadness to be leaving her friends and family. She didn't think she was ready to leave Candle Beach yet. It was something she needed to prepare for, not do on the spur-of-the-moment.

"I'm sorry, I very much appreciate the offer, but I've already committed to this project in Candle Beach. I hope you understand."

"Of course. I admire your loyalty." Vanessa cleared her throat. "If anything else comes up, I'll be sure to think of you." Someone said something on Vanessa's end of the call. "Gretchen, I've got to go. Please say hi to Dahlia for me."

"I will. Thank you again for thinking of me. Bye."

She hung up the phone, still wondering if she'd made the right decision to turn down the job. Only time would tell.

16

*G*retchen checked her reflection in the mirror and frowned at her pale skin. Splitting her time between two jobs had taken its toll. She shook her head upside down to add more body to her hair and brushed on more pink blush. She stared at the woman in the mirror. Now she looked presentable.

The sales office had closed early at two o'clock for the fourth of July. Not that they'd had many customers. Everyone was focused on getting to the beach or to a party to celebrate the holiday. In fact, she was heading somewhere herself.

Charlotte had invited her to a friend's party. At first, Gretchen had declined the offer, but Charlotte had wheedled until she got her way. Gretchen would rather have taken a nap, but she knew it would be good for her to get out of the house. She hadn't seen much of Dahlia or Maggie lately either as they'd been busy with work and family, and she badly needed a fun evening out. She made a mental note to set up a girls' night to catch up.

The carriage house's upstairs apartment heated up far

faster than her house did, and she had purchased a window air conditioning unit to cool the space down. She switched it on higher now to combat the early July temperatures.

"You should be good now, Reilly." He looked up from where he lay on the bed. His ears perked up and he hopped down and ran to the door. She petted his neck and said, "Sorry buddy, humans only today. We'll take a long walk later." He slumped to the floor. She wouldn't be surprised if she found him waiting in the same position when she returned from the party.

She grabbed a light jacket off the hook next to the door and gave him a final pet. "See you, buddy."

In the yard between the carriage house and the main house, flowers of all types bloomed. Charlotte had turned out to have quite a green thumb and she'd helped Gretchen keep the large gardens weeded and watered.

Charlotte waved at her from the main house's back porch and Gretchen tromped down the carriage house stairs to meet her.

"Hey, ready to go?" Charlotte was dressed in holiday-appropriate attire of royal blue capris and a red-and-white striped silk blouse. Gretchen felt underdressed in her denim shorts and tank top.

"Should I change?" She pulled at her clothes and checked Charlotte's reaction.

"No, you're fine. Anything goes at this party."

"You haven't told me much about it," Gretchen said. "Whose house is it at?"

"Oh, just someone I know," Charlotte said vaguely. She brushed a sprinkling of dirt from her white canvas sandals.

"Should we bring anything?" In Gretchen's family, it was customary to bring something to a gathering.

"We'll stop by the market in Haven Shores to pick something up." Charlotte unlocked her car and they both climbed in.

"Have you been to this party before?"

"Oh yeah, every year. You'll love it. The house is on the canal, so you can kayak or fish if you'd like. Mainly though, people sit around drinking and socializing. It's lots of fun."

Fun sounded fantastic to Gretchen. She rubbed her neck and leaned against the car door.

"You okay?" Charlotte asked. "You look exhausted."

"I'm fine. It's been a long day." Every day at work was a challenge. Parker had stopped actively pursuing her, but he had made it clear that he was still interested. They'd spent the summer with each of them fighting for the next sale. When a potential customer appeared, they took turns working with them, but Parker was two house sales ahead of Gretchen. She tried her best to avoid him, but working in close quarters made it difficult to keep him out of her mind.

Before she knew it, they were in Haven Shores. Charlotte parked in front of the Haven Shores Market.

"They're busy today," Gretchen remarked.

"Everyone waiting until the last minute to get their party supplies." Charlotte grinned. "Kind of like us."

They arrived back at the car in thirty minutes, their arms laden with veggie and fruit platters and a few family-sized bags of chips.

"I think we've got enough for a small army," Gretchen said.

Charlotte shoved everything into the back of her BMW sedan. "That's probably an accurate assessment of how many people will be there."

❧

A few minutes later, they pulled up in front of a mansion-like house on a large lot. A wide expanse of canal stretched out behind the house. At least thirty cars were already parked in the gravel driveway and on the side lawn.

Gretchen's eyes widened. "Whose house is this?" She'd grown up in an upper middle class family, but this was money, more than she'd ever imagined.

Charlotte shrugged. "Just someone I know."

They carried the food into the house and set it down on an expansive marble countertop spanning half the length of the air-conditioned kitchen. Gretchen raised her eyebrows. Platters of food filled every available space. Near the back door was a white insulated cooler filled with drinks.

Charlotte walked over to the cooler and opened it up. "Beer, soda, wine cooler or water?"

"A wine cooler sounds great." She took it from Charlotte's hand and unscrewed the cap. Charlotte pulled out a Diet Pepsi and opened the door to the back deck.

A blast of warm air hit them. She half wished she could stay inside the cool kitchen, but the sound of laughter drew her out.

"Charlotte," a well-dressed man in his fifties called out as soon as they set foot on the deck. He looked like an older version of Parker.

"Is this your parents' house?" Gretchen hissed to Charlotte.

"Yes." Charlotte blushed. "It's their annual fourth of July party."

"Why didn't you tell me?" The man had separated from his conversation partner and was walking toward them. Did he know who she was? What would happen if they found out she was Eliza and Daniel Roberts' daughter?

"I knew you wouldn't come if you knew," Charlotte said.

"You're right." Her mind whirled trying to figure out how she'd get home. Haven Shores had a few taxis, but they'd probably be booked with holiday traffic.

"Does he know who I am? Who my parents are?"

"No, he doesn't know."

Charlotte's father was upon them. He wrapped his arm around Charlotte and then assessed Gretchen.

"And who is your friend?"

"This is Gretchen. She owns the house I'm renting in Candle Beach." Charlotte smiled at Gretchen. "Gretchen, this is my dad, Barry. Dad, this is Gretchen."

"Nice to meet you," Barry said. Then a man tapped him on the arm and muttered a few words to him. He nodded.

"Sorry girls, I've got to take care of something. Gretchen, it was so nice to meet you. I'll have to get up to Candle Beach sometime soon. Charlotte raves about the marvelous view of the ocean from your house."

"And you need to see Whimsical Delights too," Charlotte added.

"Yes, of course." He waved goodbye before striding off across the lawn.

"He hasn't seen your boutique?"

"No, he's been really busy this summer." Her smile slipped, but she quickly recovered. "It's okay, I'm still working out the kinks at the shop."

"And he doesn't know who you're renting from?"

"It's never come up." Charlotte grinned innocently.

A thought occurred to Gretchen. If this was Charlotte's parents' house, would Parker be there? After weighing the pros and cons of the job in Seattle, she'd realized she didn't want to give up on a future with him. Her date with Adam had taught her she wasn't as over Parker as she had thought, and with so many things left unsaid between them, this wasn't the right time to leave Candle Beach. If things didn't work out with him, she could still move later. She scanned the crowd. No sign of him.

"Who are you looking for?" Charlotte asked. "Parker?"

"Yes."

"Don't worry, he's not planning on coming tonight. He's been working so much, he wanted to have some time off to himself to relax."

"I know the feeling." Gretchen sipped from her wine cooler to hide her disappointment. She'd hoped he'd be there so they could talk, but she didn't want to alert Charlotte.

"Let me introduce you to some people." Charlotte tugged on her arm and pulled her over to a group of people chatting next to a fire pit.

Several hours later, she had to admit she was glad she'd accepted the party invitation. She'd met a lot of people and even pitched Oceanview Estates to a few people who had asked about it when she'd told them where she worked.

She plopped herself down in a woven plastic lounge chair facing the canal and downed half a bottle of water. The sun hung low in the sky, but still provided warmth. She lay back and closed her eyes behind her sunglasses, tuning out the rest of the world.

Things were going better than she'd expected at work. Martin seemed pleased with their sales progress. Even her mother had directed a few new clients to her from Candle Beach Real Estate. With her commission checks and Charlotte's rent payments, she should be able to move to Seattle before winter if she chose to do so.

Recently, the thought of moving had exhilarated her, but also caused twinges of anxiety and sadness. Candle Beach had been her home for so long. Was she ready to leave all of her family and friends behind?

As if on cue, someone tapped her on the shoulder. Her eyes flew open and adrenaline shot through her system.

"Sorry, I didn't mean to startle you. You looked so peaceful that I wasn't even sure if I should bother you, but I wanted to say hi." Parker smiled at her. He'd changed out of his normal work uniform of khaki pants and a polo shirt and was dressed in informal cargo shorts and a t-shirt. He carried a plastic plate with brownies on it.

"Hi." She sat up and removed her sunglasses to see him better in the dimming light. He'd come to the party after all. She'd met so many new people that her nerves were on edge and seeing a familiar face soothed them. But now it was do or die time. Did she have the guts to tell him how she felt about him?

To break the ice, she motioned to the brownies and said, "I see you're getting your chocolate fix in."

"I am." He grinned. "Want some?"

She shook her head. "No thanks, I already had a few. I'm surprised to see you here. Charlotte said you weren't going to be able to make it."

"I changed my mind." He grinned the easy smile that made her melt. "I was hoping you'd be here."

Her heart skipped a beat. "I was hoping you would be here too." She glanced up at him and took a deep breath. "I wanted to have a chance to talk with you."

"About what?" He sat on the edge of the lounger and put down his plate.

"I had a job offer in Seattle."

"Oh. Are you going to take it?" he asked. "Wait, had? As in past tense?"

"Yes, had. I turned it down."

"Why would you do that? That's all you've talked about since I met you. Getting to Seattle and starting a new life." He stared at her, incredulous.

"I didn't want to leave Candle Beach so soon." She took another deep breath and mumbled, "Or leave you."

He scooted closer. "You didn't want to leave me?"

"Yes."

"Are you saying what I think you're saying?" His voice rose. "You'll give me another chance?"

"I think so." She swung her legs around so that she was facing him and searched his eyes. "Is that okay with you?"

"Of course." He pulled her close and kissed her temple. "What made you change your mind? Not that I'm questioning your decision." He laid feathery kisses along her hairline and his fingers traced the contours of her face. She tilted her head and sighed.

"You. No matter how hard I tried, I couldn't stop thinking of you." She smiled at him and laced her fingers through his thick hair. "I may have ended things too hastily."

She kissed him firmly on the mouth. He tasted like chocolate, reminding her of the day they met at the Candle Beach Chocolate Festival. She'd never have imagined then that they'd be here, together, so many months later.

He hungrily returned her kiss, his hands roving up and down her back. His touch sent chills along her spine and furthered her desire. This was even better than she'd remembered. They'd wasted so much time apart that they could have spent together. True, he'd been a distraction at work, but she needed to get past that and figure out how to blend her personal and professional lives. Being single forever wasn't a viable option.

The sky darkened around them. His hands wrapped

around her waist and he lifted her onto his lap. She circled his neck with her arms and pressed herself against him as closely as she could. She never wanted this magical feeling to end.

Too soon, the sound of people passing them on the way down to the canal jolted her out of the moment. She broke their embrace, hopping off his lap and blushing furiously. "I hope no one saw us."

"So what if they did." He waggled his eyebrows and she laughed. He was right. Who cared if people saw them? Kissing him had felt too good.

He stood and reached for her hand, entwining his fingers through hers. She rubbed the pad of her thumb across his rough skin, sending more pings of desire through her already alert system.

"To be continued later," he said as he reached for her other hand and kissed her again, this time sweetly. "The fireworks should be starting soon. My parents usually put on a show and we can see the fireworks in town from here too."

He looked behind her and blanched. "In fact, we should get going before all the good seats are taken." He released one hand and tugged at the other to get her to follow.

His abrupt action caused her to pause. He'd gone from loving to panicked in less than thirty seconds. Why was he acting so strangely?

A woman's voice cut through the darkness. "There you are. You've been hiding from me." She came close enough for Gretchen to see her face.

17

*P*arker pulled Gretchen close. "Hi, Mom." He sighed. This was not going to end well.

"Parker." His mother narrowed her eyes at him.

Gretchen gave him a questioning look.

"I believe you've met," he said dryly. "Gretchen, this is my mother, Denise."

Gretchen's eyes ping-ponged between them. "This is your mom?"

The color drained from her face and then she flushed. He could see her drawing her own conclusions. She turned to Denise.

"You're the woman from Starbucks. Why didn't you say anything to me then? Did you know who I was all along?"

Denise had the good grace to look guilty. "I didn't know to start. But you told me your name and I put two and two together."

"And you!" She whipped around to face Parker. "Did she tell you about the job at Oceanview Estates? Is that why you interviewed for it?"

Denise took a few steps back. "I'll leave you two to figure things out alone." She scurried away.

Parker turned his gaze back to Gretchen. "Yes, she told me about meeting you. But she didn't know we were dating."

Gretchen looked as crushed as she'd been the day of her first interview. In a soft voice, she said, "So she told you about the job and you went after it, even though you knew I was in the running for it?"

"No, that's not what happened. I care about you, I'd never do that to you."

Her voice was hard. "But you did." Tears sprouted from her eyes and she started to walk away.

"Gretchen, wait." He held out his arms to her.

She turned back to him. "Leave me alone. I don't want to have anything to do with you."

In the distance, fireworks burst into colorful formations in the air and the crowd cheered. None of that mattered. All he could do was watch helplessly as Gretchen walked away from him. Things had been going so well, but as he'd feared, the secret he'd kept from her had torn them apart.

"I need to go home," Gretchen said to Charlotte. She'd been looking for her in the dark for ten minutes and had finally found her watching the fireworks.

"Now?" Charlotte motioned to the display. "But it's not over yet."

"I need to go now." She choked on her words and Charlotte looked at her closer, seeming to finally notice the tears that streamed down her face.

"Okay," Charlotte said. She grabbed Gretchen's arm.

"What happened? Did Parker say something that upset you? I heard he was here."

"No. It wasn't something he said today. It was something he didn't tell me when we were dating." She sobbed and leaned against her friend.

"What did he do? He's my brother, but if he did something awful to you, I'm going to kick his butt."

Gretchen didn't answer and Charlotte led her wordlessly to the car. She waited until they were on the road back to Candle Beach before she resumed her inquisition.

"So what did he do?"

Gretchen sighed and leaned against the window. Talking about Parker to his sister wasn't high on her list of fun things to do. "Your mother told him about the job at Oceanview Estates. She found out about it from me. That's the only reason he interviewed for the position. He probably lied to me about everything from the start."

Charlotte looked at her sideways. "Are you sure? That doesn't sound like my brother."

"He admitted that she told him about the job."

"Hmm." Charlotte stared straight ahead. "I still can't believe it. Parker is one of the most honest people I know."

"Yeah, well, obviously you don't know him as well as you think." Gretchen sighed and slumped in her seat. "I don't want to talk about it. Can we talk about it later?"

"Sure." Charlotte drove them home in silence.

Gretchen drove to work the next day dreading the idea of seeing Parker. How could she possibly work with him after what he'd done to her? For about the millionth time in the last twelve hours, she wished she hadn't given up the job in Seattle that Dahlia's mom had offered her.

What had she been thinking? She'd put her heart out there and it had been stomped on, just as it had been every time before. The best thing to do would have been to accept the job in Seattle, graciously tell Martin that she wanted to quit her sales position and move on with life outside of Candle Beach. Now, none of that was an option.

She pushed open the door of the model home. Parker was at his desk, engrossed in something on his computer. He looked up and started to rise.

"Gretchen."

"Don't." Her lips formed a thin line as she seated herself behind her desk without looking at him.

He didn't respect her wishes. "Can I explain to you what really happened?"

"I know what happened." She finally looked at him. "You betrayed my trust."

"I know," he said. "But I want to explain."

"I don't want to hear it." She shuffled some papers around on her desk, but couldn't focus on the words through her blurred vision.

"Please let me explain it to you."

"No, we're done. We're not dating, we're not friends, we're nothing."

He sighed. "Fine. But we need to figure out our work relationship."

"We come to work. You sell houses to your customers and I sell to mine."

He paused for a moment and then narrowed his eyes. "Look, if you won't listen to what I have to say and you want us to be nothing more than co-workers, things are going to change around here."

"Like what?" What was he talking about?

"Like I take any clients that approach me first—no more of this taking turns business."

It was Gretchen's turn to stare. "But your desk is closest to the entrance."

"Yeah, well, you chose your desk."

She jutted out her chin. "I'm not worried."

"Oh, but you should be. I'm not pulling any punches anymore." He stalked out the room.

Later that day, while Parker was out checking on a building lot with another customer, Natalie showed up with a man, presumably her husband. He was in his early fifties and dressed in the same informal yet dressy style as his wife.

Natalie scanned the room and her eyes lit on Gretchen. Gretchen smiled and walked toward the couple with her right hand outstretched.

"Natalie, it's nice to see you again."

"Hi, Gretchen, this is my husband Steve. He finally was able to get off work and look at some of the properties with me."

"Nice to meet you." She firmly shook Steve's hand. "Well, let's get out there." She led them out the door. She crossed her fingers that Parker wouldn't be in view of the Cliffside properties. Natalie had come in a few times since Gretchen had met her just after Memorial Day. She'd worked with both of them, and they had agreed that whoever was with the customer on the day she put an offer in would get the commission.

It looked like today might be that day, since Natalie had brought her husband with her. If she could keep Parker away, she may nab the biggest commission in the whole development. The three of them approached the Cliffside properties. Behind one of the houses under construction,

Parker stood with his client. He appeared to be pointing out the view and different aspects of the construction.

"Steve, this is the lot I've been looking at." Natalie motioned to one of the larger Cliffside lots. From here, the view was astounding. With the sun shining down, the gentle ocean breeze and the seagulls chattering in the distance, Gretchen couldn't have asked for a better day to make a sale.

The couple spent the next half hour assessing the site. Finally, Steve nodded in approval. "I like it."

Natalie beamed and grabbed his arm. "I told you it was perfect."

"You were right." He patted his wife's arm and looked at Gretchen. "I think we're ready to make an offer. I believe my wife has picked out a floor plan for this site?"

She grinned, unable to completely hide her excitement. Yes! She'd hoped today would be the day. How fortunate that Parker wasn't able to be present. She glanced down the hill toward the half-built house where she'd last seen Parker. He wasn't there anymore.

"Looking for someone?"

She spun around and her grin faded.

"Hello, Parker," Natalie said. "I'm glad you were here so I could introduce my husband to you."

She turned to her husband. "Steve, this is Parker, the one I've told you so much about. He has so many ideas for the exterior of our new house."

"Ah yes, Parker. It's nice to meet you. My wife has spoken of you often. I assume you'll be a part of our team as we build?"

Parker shot Gretchen a cat-got-the-canary grin.

"Of course. I'll be with you every step of the way."

She turned away for a moment, pretending to check something on her phone. Inside, she fumed. Where had he come from, and how had he known she was there? He shouldn't have been able to see them from the house he'd been at with his client. Losing this commission would hurt. She turned back to the group.

"Of course he'll be part of the team." Gretchen smiled at Natalie and Steve. "We're all one big family here, right Parker?" He nodded, and smiled with his lips pressed tightly together.

She brushed her hands together. "Now, let's get back to the sales office and write up that contract."

"Sounds good." Steve grabbed his wife's hand and smiled tenderly at her before nudging her to get her attention. He whispered to her, "We're going to get our dream house, honey." Natalie gazed up at him and grinned.

Gretchen turned away from the intimate moment and quickened her pace to allow them some privacy. This was obviously something the couple had wanted for a while. They'd probably been through a lot before getting to the stage of buying a million-dollar home on the ocean together. She wondered if she'd ever have the chance to experience the glances of love that they exchanged.

As if on cue, Parker bumped against her. At this point, they were out of earshot of their customers. "So how are we going to split this commission?" he asked.

"What do you mean? I was helping Natalie on the day she made the offer, so the commission is mine. That's what we'd discussed previously."

"That's what we talked about when I was under the assumption that we were friends. We need to split the commission." His eyes shot daggers at her.

"Fine, we'll split it fifty-fifty." She put her hands on her hips.

"No. I want seventy percent."

She stopped and stared at him. "What are you talking about? Fifty percent to each of us is fair. We both put work into this sale."

"They came here for me," he said. "You heard Natalie. I've been working with her on their home's design elements."

"But I met her first. You stole her from me."

"I didn't steal the client. By her account, you couldn't even find a floor plan to show her. She wanted someone who could actually be helpful." He crossed his arms across his chest.

Gretchen reeled backwards. She didn't like the new Parker. On the other hand, it made it easier to not fantasize about what his arms had felt like when he'd held her tightly against his chest. "No, this is my client. Fifty-fifty is how we're going to split it."

"Is something wrong?" Natalie frowned at them. They'd been stopped for so long that their customers had caught up to them.

"Nothing's wrong." Parker relaxed his stance. "We were discussing some of the construction details for another project."

"Good, now let's get started on our house," Steve said. They walked in silence back to the sales office. He held the door open for his wife and followed her inside. Gretchen stopped to remove a rock from her sandal.

Parker hesitated at the door. "Gretchen, are you coming?" His tone was purely professional, holding none of the warmth that he used to exhibit toward her.

18

September

"Well, if it isn't my two favorite sales agents," Martin's voice boomed from the doorway of the model home. A draft from the open door ruffled the floor plans on the kitchen counter.

Parker met him near the entrance. "Martin, hey. Nice to see you." He clapped him on the shoulder.

His boss hadn't been in for a while, which Parker hoped meant he was pleased with the work they were doing. Since their break-up on the fourth of July, he and Gretchen had spoken no more than absolutely necessary. It hurt him to see her acting that way, but she'd made it clear that she didn't trust him and there would never be anything romantic between them. He'd decided that it was time to move on and focus on his career like he'd intended to do. His dedication showed. In the last few months, he'd sold more houses than he'd ever thought possible.

"Hi Martin," Gretchen said, coming up to him to shake

his hand. "What's going on? Did you see your house? It's almost finished. It'll be gorgeous when it's done."

"I did," he said. "My wife is coming out here next week to pick out the finishing touches. She's so excited and truth be told, so am I. I may even decide to slow down a bit so we can enjoy the beach house together."

"You deserve it." She smiled at him.

"Did you get the sales numbers I sent you?" Parker asked.

"I did. Congratulations, you two. I knew I'd picked a winning team when I chose both of you to helm the ship. The development is selling out faster than my predictions. At this rate, we'll be done by winter." He eyed them. "In fact, that's why I'm here. I thought I'd provide an incentive to sell out by December."

Parker's ears perked up at the mention of an incentive. The sales job had been profitable, but the start-up costs for a new real estate firm would be significant. Every little bit helped.

"So, to sweeten the deal, whichever of you sells the most houses by December, or whenever the development is fully sold, will earn a bonus equal to your average commission." Martin beamed at them. "Does that sound good to you?"

Parker recovered first. "Yes, that sounds great. Thank you, Martin."

Gretchen nodded. "It's more than generous. We won't disappoint you. Thank you."

Martin left, leaving the two of them to stare at each other.

"May the best man win." Parker crossed his arms and leaned against the counter.

"Or woman," she corrected. She balled her fists and turned haughtily around to retreat to her desk.

Game on, he thought.

~

October

Reilly's barks woke Gretchen from a deep sleep. She opened one eye. He was sitting on the bed next to her, holding his leash in his mouth. She opened the other eye and rubbed the sleep from the corners of her eyelids. He dropped the leash and licked her face.

Ugh. She sat up and a wave of dizziness swept over her. She flopped back down on the pillow and Reilly barked again. What time was it anyways? And why was she still wearing yesterday's clothes?

She looked at her alarm clock. Almost nine o'clock? No wonder her dog was so anxious to get outside. She'd felt rotten the night before and had crashed on her bed as soon as she'd returned home from work. She must have forgotten to set the alarm.

Shoot! Work! She'd be late to work. Her head swam. Where was she supposed to be today? What day was it? She glanced at the calendar across the room. It was Thursday and she was due at Candle Beach Real Estate in twenty minutes.

She sat up again and this time was able to put her feet on the floor. Her throat felt like someone had scraped the inside with industrial-grade sandpaper. When she stood, every muscle in her body protested. This was not going to be a fun day at work.

She opened the door and Reilly trotted over to it.

"Sorry buddy, no long walk today." She shooed him out to the yard and threw on some clothes from her clean laundry basket.

Her reflection in the mirror showed dark bags under her eyes, raw skin under her nose and an overall pallor. Yeah, this was going to go over great with her clients. There was nothing she could do though. To make her dream of moving to Seattle a reality, she couldn't afford to miss any work. She needed every bit of money she could earn.

She herded Reilly back to her apartment and grabbed her keys. Ordinarily, she'd walk into Candle Beach for work, but with the way she felt, she may not even make it halfway down the hill, much less back up the hill to her house after work. She held tightly to the railing of the carriage house's outer stairs and picked her way down to the alley. Reilly trotted after her, excited to be leaving the confines of the small apartment to go to doggy daycare.

"Hey, Gretchen." Charlotte glanced up from where she was kneeling on a foam pad in the garden. She held a small gardening shovel in her hand. "How's it going?" She looked closer at Gretchen. "Are you okay?"

"I'm fine," she lied. "Just didn't get enough sleep."

Charlotte stood and brushed the dirt off her frayed jeans. "You're staggering." She eyed her friend. "And you look like a truck ran over you."

"I feel like a whole fleet of Mack trucks ran over me," she admitted. "But I can't go back to bed."

Charlotte walked over and put her hand on Gretchen's shoulder. "You can't keep burning the midnight oil." She pushed her back toward the carriage house.

"Where are you supposed to be today?" Charlotte asked.

"Candle Beach Real Estate."

"I'll call and let them know you aren't going to be in today."

"But I have to," she protested weakly as she let Charlotte guide her up the stairs.

Gretchen unlocked the door and Reilly shot past her to get inside, bouncing around under his leash hanging by the door. She used her legs to push him back inside, but even that effort exhausted her. She collapsed on the small loveseat.

"Do you want some tea?" Charlotte asked.

"Don't you have to get to work?"

"Eh." She shrugged. "That's the benefit of owning my own business. I only have myself to answer to. Besides, it's after Labor Day and weekdays aren't very busy." She busied herself with the teakettle on the stove. "What kind of tea do you want?"

"Chamomile. Thanks." Gretchen bundled herself up on the couch with an afghan. Reilly jumped up on her feet and laid his head on her knees.

"You need a bigger couch," Charlotte said.

She smiled faintly. "This is big enough for me and Reilly." Charlotte handed her the mug of hot water and she dunked the chamomile tea bag into it. "Thanks for the tea, but I'm fine, really. You can go."

"Okay, but I'm coming by at lunch to check on you."

Charlotte closed the door behind her, leaving Gretchen alone.

She looked around. The carriage house apartment felt claustrophobic. She wasn't there very often during the day and usually didn't notice how small it was. She hoped her future apartment in Seattle would be larger.

A little after noon, Charlotte came back with a to-go container of soup from the Bluebonnet Café.

"Maggie recommended the chicken noodle." She set the soup on the coffee table in front of Gretchen. "She said she'd come check on you tomorrow. Oh, and your mom said not to worry about missing work today."

"I'd better be feeling a lot better by tomorrow. I can't miss my shift at Oceanview Estates." She and Parker were neck and neck in sales and she wasn't going to let him win the bonus commission.

"I'm sure it would be fine if you did. I can call Parker to cover if necessary."

"No!" Gretchen shouted. She kicked off the afghan and tried to stand. Her legs gave out from under her and she flopped back on the couch.

Charlotte touched her forehead. "You're burning up. Where's your thermometer?"

Gretchen told her where it was and Charlotte gave it to her to use.

"102.5," Gretchen said, handing the thermometer back.

"Yeah, you're not going anywhere tomorrow."

Gretchen glared at her, folded her arms over her chest and went back to watching the small TV attached to a metal arm sticking out from the wall. Charlotte sighed and left.

The next day, Gretchen awoke feeling just as bad as the day before. *I've got to get to work though, otherwise Parker will have an edge on me*, she thought. Reilly looked at her hopefully, but she couldn't do any more than let him outside for a few minutes. If she took him to doggy daycare, she'd never have enough energy to make it into work. At lunchtime, she'd come home to let him out again. She forced herself to dress in something reasonably professional and descended the stairs as fast as she dared. If she could make it to her car in time, she could avoid another confrontation with Charlotte.

She was backing her car into the alley when Charlotte appeared at the back door of the big house. She tipped her head to the side as if trying to assess Gretchen's health through the car windshield. She scrambled down the steps and jogged toward the car. Gretchen waved and drove off before she could reach her. In the rearview mirror, she saw her standing in the alley, frowning, with her hands on her hips. She'd deal with the wrath of her friend when she returned. The important thing was, she was going to make it in to work today, sick or not.

She parked in her usual space around the corner from the sales office. So many houses had been built or were under construction that it no longer looked like a sales office in the middle of an empty parking lot. Instead, it looked like what it actually was—a model home in the middle of a residential development.

When she walked in the door and trudged over to her desk, Parker stared at her in surprise.

"Charlotte said you were at death's door. I didn't expect to see you in here today."

"I have a job to do." She coughed. Her throat tickled and she started coughing uncontrollably.

"Would you like a glass of water?" He nodded toward the kitchen. Before she could answer, he pushed back his chair and stood.

She glared at him. "I can get it myself." She walked over to the kitchen and retrieved a glass from the cupboard. As she ran water into the glass, she had to prop herself up on the edge of the sink. In truth, it had taken all the energy she had to get to work and walk into the building.

"Okay. Sorry I asked." Parker returned to his desk, but she could feel his eyes on her.

She almost hoped that there wouldn't be much business that day. But luck was not on her side. A potential customer came into the sales office while Parker was on the phone with one of his clients. She waved at the man and he came over to her desk and sat down across from her.

She introduced herself and asked a few questions to find out what he was looking for. After determining he was looking for a smaller three-bedroom house, she showed him some plans.

"Here you go. I think you'll like the Oceanscape plan."

The man took the paper from her and reviewed it. She watched him and felt a sneeze coming on. She tried to hold it back, but that only made it worse. The sneeze erupted from her, spraying the entire desk, including the floor plan in front of him.

Her eyes widened.

"I'm so sorry," she said to the man. He appeared at a loss for words. She quickly gathered up all the papers and swept them into the recycling bin underneath her desk. The effort caused another coughing fit. The man looked at her in horror, thanked her for her time and scurried out of the building.

She put her head down on the desk. What she wouldn't give at the moment for a soft pillow and her own bed. Footsteps echoed on the floor next to her.

"You've got to go home. You aren't in any shape to be here." Parker's face was contorted with concern.

"No, I've got to be here," she mumbled. She couldn't bring herself to remove her head from the desk.

"You're scaring away potential clients."

Parker was right. She shouldn't be there. A tear slipped out of her eye, followed by a torrent of tears.

He pulled up a chair. "Gretch, it's okay. Everyone gets sick. You need to go home and rest."

She lifted her head and tried to focus on his face. His expression was much kinder than she'd expected.

"But I have to make this work," she blubbered.

"One day..." Parker assessed her and amended his statement, "or maybe a few days, at home won't derail your career." He handed her a tissue from her desk. "C'mon. I'll take you home. You're in no shape to be driving."

"But you can't leave the sales office with no one here."

"It'll only take thirty minutes to drop you off at home and come back. No big deal. Let's go." He gently pulled her up, grabbed her purse from below the desk and nudged her out the door to his car. "When you're feeling better, I'll have Charlotte drive you here to get your car."

"Okay." As soon as she said that, she felt much better. He made a quick phone call and drove her home.

When they arrived at her house, Charlotte ran out to meet the car. "I told you not to go anywhere," she chided.

Gretchen was too tired to argue. "I just want to go to bed."

Charlotte waved goodbye to Parker and helped her up the stairs. She made a beeline for her bed and Reilly jumped up on the mattress next to her, ready to serve his mistress. She laid her hand on his rough fur coat and sank into the embrace of her comfy bed.

"I'll leave you to get some sleep," Charlotte said. "But I'll be back later to check on you."

Once Charlotte was gone, Gretchen lay in bed, exhausted but not able to sleep. She never got sick like this. Even as a child, she rarely caught a cold and had escaped the stomach flu when everyone else around her had it. Her mother joked that she had a golden immune system.

So what was going on now? She knew the answer. Charlotte was right. She was burning the candle at both ends, and something had to give. But what? She couldn't back out of working for her parents—they still needed the few days a week she could give them. And she definitely couldn't leave Oceanview Estates before all the houses were sold. How would that look to Martin?

I'll figure it out as soon as I'm feeling better, she vowed. She closed her eyes and immediately fell into a deep sleep with Reilly snuggled up against her.

19

Early November

It seemed like only yesterday that Dahlia had announced her engagement, but it was already time for Maggie and Gretchen to be fitted for their bridesmaid dresses. Gretchen had anticipated their girls' day for a while. She needed a day off to relax and laugh a little. It seemed like she'd been getting sick every other week from stress.

The owner of the bridal shop in Haven Shores appeared carrying a tray of champagne.

"Yes, please," Gretchen said. They all reached for a glass.

"Cheers," they toasted.

Gretchen drained her glass quickly, hoping the alcohol would help her relax.

"Girls, are you ready?" Dahlia's eyes twinkled.

"Are the dresses hideous?" Gretchen asked.

"Gretchen!" Maggie admonished. "She didn't mean it, Dahlia."

"I did mean it." She laughed. "I'll wear whatever you want me to wear for your wedding, but if it's ugly, it's not going in my closet. Space is at a premium in the carriage house."

Dahlia walked over to a hanging rack concealed by one of the floor-to-ceiling mirrors.

"Ta-da!" She held up two yellow and green dresses, covered with yards of ruffles.

Gretchen's face twisted in dismay before she could hide her reaction.

"Those are, um, very interesting," Maggie eked out.

"What, you don't like them?" Dahlia burst out laughing.

"You are joking, right?" She eyed the dresses.

"Yes, of course. Did you really think I'd be that mean?" Dahlia replaced the dresses on the rack and pulled out two long garment bags. "These are your real dresses." She removed the plastic covering from one and showed them the dress.

Gretchen's eyes widened. "It's gorgeous." She reached out to touch the satin dress.

"This one's yours." Dahlia handed it to Gretchen and gave Maggie the other garment bag.

"Ooh." Maggie grabbed it from Dahlia.

"Go try it on," she urged.

They came out of the dressing room and twirled in front of the three full-length mirrors.

"I look so pretty," Maggie said as she admired herself in the mirror. A flowing, floor-length skirt fell from a tight bodice and thick straps. The dark violet color highlighted Maggie's red hair and blue eyes.

"Mine seems a little big." Gretchen plucked at wads of extra fabric in the waistline.

Dahlia checked the label. "It's a size eight, just like you

requested. But you're right, it's way too big." The dress hung on her like a flour sack.

The owner came in and frowned at Gretchen. "You need something a few sizes smaller. It's too loose to alter properly. We'll have to get you another dress."

"I ordered these over the summer." Dahlia looked closer at her friend's pale face. "Are you okay, Gretchen?"

Maggie chimed in, "Yeah, you've lost a lot of weight and you didn't have much to lose. Is everything okay?"

It was too much. Tears streamed down Gretchen's face. "I'm fine, really," she blubbered. Maggie handed her a Kleenex out of her purse.

Dahlia sat down next to Gretchen and put her arm around her. "What's going on?"

"It's work and Parker and everything. I haven't had a day off in months and Parker won't talk to me unless it's absolutely necessary for work."

"Isn't that what you wanted?" Dahlia asked. "You told him to leave you alone."

"Yeah," Gretchen admitted. "But I didn't realize how horrible it would be at work without having anyone to talk to. I feel so alone, at work and at home in my tiny apartment."

Maggie put her hands on Gretchen's shoulders. "Honey, it's okay. We all feel like that sometimes, right Dahlia?"

Dahlia nodded. "This summer was tough for me too. I was so busy with the bookstore that I didn't have time for anyone else, much less myself."

Gretchen dried her tears and tried to steel herself. She was ruining Dahlia's special day at the dress shop.

"You've got to slow down." Maggie fished a new Kleenex out of her purse and handed it to her. "Isn't the development almost sold out? Maybe you could quit now? That would help with your stress levels, especially with the Parker situation."

"I can't quit now." She wiped her eyes. "We're so close to selling out the development. I can't leave those commissions behind. I need the money."

"While I can't say I'm too keen that you're leaving Candle Beach, I get where you're coming from," Dahlia said. "But your health and emotional well-being is important too." Maggie nodded in agreement.

"I almost have enough saved. It's something I have to do for myself. I can't work for my parents for the rest of my life. If nothing else, working at Oceanview Estates has shown me how great it is to succeed on my own."

Maggie looked sad.

"Well, we'll miss you." Dahlia hugged her.

"Enough about me," Gretchen said. "This is your day." She walked into the changing room and slipped out of the dress. Through the closed door, she said, "Time to move on to the main event. Let's see your dress." She burst out of the main room to see her friends whispering between themselves. "What?"

Maggie and Dahlia exchanged guilty glances.

"Nothing." Dahlia rose from the couch and set her champagne glass down on the end table. "I'd love to show you my dress."

She disappeared into the dressing room and the owner of the bridal shop followed to help her into the dress. Gretchen and Maggie made small talk while Dahlia changed.

Ten minutes later, she emerged, wearing a spectacularly beautiful dress.

"Wow," Gretchen said. Her friend had been transformed from her normal casual attire. "You look like a princess."

The white satin dress was embellished with white beads that covered the strapless bodice, and a full skirt billowed out.

Maggie gazed at her friend. "Show us the back."

Dahlia spun slowly around, beaming at her reflection in the mirror. The dress was long in the back, with a short train.

"See, I can bustle it up with this button," Dahlia said. The attendant held the train up to her and she showed them how it buttoned to form an ankle-length dress. "I'll be able to dance in it."

"It's perfect," Maggie said. "You and your mom chose the most perfect dress possible for you." Dahlia and her mother had gone dress shopping in Seattle and had the dress shipped to Haven Shores for alterations.

"I know, right?" Dahlia said. "I couldn't even recall what it looked like; it's been a few months since we picked it out." She twirled again. "But it's even more beautiful than I remembered."

"Garrett is going to flip out when he sees it," Gretchen said.

"No kidding," Maggie said. "He's lucky to have you."

"I know," Dahlia joked. "I tell him that every day." Her expression turned dreamy. "But I'm getting a pretty good guy myself."

"You are," Gretchen agreed. "I hope I find someone like Garrett."

"He's got a cousin who's flying in for the wedding," Dahlia said. "I've heard he's quite attractive."

"Well, I still think Parker is the guy for you." Maggie met Gretchen's eyes through their reflections in the mirror.

"I think that ship has sailed." Gretchen stood to examine Dahlia's veil. It was embroidered with slivers of white silk ribbons and the same beads that adorned the dress.

"Maybe, maybe not," Maggie said.

"He lied to me. I don't know if I can ever forgive that," Gretchen said. "And I don't need a man in my life right now. What I need to do is take charge of my career."

"You know, there was a time in my life when I felt the same way." Dahlia lifted the train and preened in front of the mirror.

"Yeah, like last year," Maggie said.

"Exactly. I swore Garrett wasn't the right man for me and I wasn't ever going to let a man influence my decisions ever again. I also said I wasn't going to stay in Candle Beach." She shrugged and a far-off look came into her eyes. "But you know what? Sometimes what we envision for ourselves isn't what we really need."

"It worked out for you and Garrett, and I'm glad it did," Gretchen said. "But that doesn't mean that all relationships are meant to be. Sometimes you have to let things go."

They were all quiet for a moment. Maggie stared into her half-full champagne glass and Dahlia pretended to smooth out a wrinkle.

Dahlia broke the silence. "Well, I've got to get out of this thing before I spill champagne on it." The owner helped her into the dressing room, leaving Maggie alone with Dahlia.

"Sorry if we keep bugging you about Parker," Maggie said quietly.

"I know you mean well, but it's time to give up. It's never going to happen." Her mood had been sinking since she'd tried on her bridesmaid dress. She stood. "I think I'm going to take off now," she said.

"But we were going to have dinner together in Haven Shores," Maggie said. "Dahlia will be disappointed."

"I know. Please tell her I'm sorry, but with the way I'm feeling, I don't think I'd make very good company."

She'd looked forward to this day with her friends, but now it felt as miserable as every day had been since she started her quest to leave Candle Beach. Doubts about her future swirled through her mind. Was her misery a sign that leaving Candle Beach to strike out on her own wasn't in her best interest? Should she leave Oceanview Estates before completion? She didn't want to do that, but her friends were right. The stress of having two jobs was wearing on her and she couldn't take much more of it.

Gretchen hadn't worked up the nerve to tell Martin she wanted to quit. That, or she didn't want to quit. She hadn't decided yet. It seemed silly to quit working now when the project was so close to completion. Only a few of the lots in the Cliffside section were left for sale.

She put her head down on her desk. She'd been there since seven a.m., catching up on some paperwork that she hadn't finished before she left for her dress fitting. The long days were killing her and insomnia had struck in the last week. A moment of rest before potential customers came in sounded wonderful.

"Gretchen," Parker's commanding voice woke her up. She lifted her head from the desk. "Were you sleeping?" he asked.

"No, just resting my eyes for a moment. I got here early." What time was it anyways? She looked at the clock on the wall and groaned. No wonder Parker was here—it was nine o'clock already. Her short rest had turned into an hour-long snooze. She gulped some cold coffee and shuffled some papers around on her desk.

"A few more properties to sell and we'll be done," he remarked.

"Yep." She went to the kitchen and poured herself a cup of coffee. She hesitated at the coffeepot, unsure of whether she should offer him a cup. Things continued to be strained between them. She set the pot back in the coffee maker and returned to her desk.

A car in the driveway caught her attention. "Natalie's here for her walk-thru."

"Excellent. I saw the construction foreman out there when I came in and he said everything was ready. I can handle it, you don't need to come with."

"Natalie was my client first. I'm going to be there too." Under her breath, she grumbled, "It's bad enough I have to split the commission with you."

Parker turned back to her. "Did you say something?"

"No, I'll be right there." She straightened the papers on her desk and followed him out to meet with Natalie and Steve.

When they returned, the tension between them was as thick as the concrete being poured in the driveway next to the model home.

"Looks like I'm in the lead for sales." He held up a sheaf of papers.

"What? You were one house behind me."

"Yeah, and you were gone yesterday afternoon."

"You sold two houses in one day?" She stared at him with her hands on her hips.

A smug smile crept across his face. "I did. An older couple came in yesterday and bought a house for themselves and another for their adult son's family. They wanted a compound of vacation homes."

"You're kidding." Why couldn't she get the customers like that?

"No, not kidding. There are only three properties left. And I intend to sell at least two of those and win the bonus Martin promised."

Her heart sank. She'd been counting on the sales bonus as she'd been in the lead for a few weeks. What good was all the hours she'd put in if it wasn't enough to win the big commission bonus? She straightened. There was still time. She and Parker were currently tied. If she could get two out of the last three sales, she'd win.

"We'll see about that," she said.

As soon as she uttered the words, a car pulled into the driveway. They looked at each other then both ran for the door, jostling each other en route.

When they got outside, they slowed to a speed walk toward the potential customer.

A man got out of the car and approached Parker first. Parker flashed a grin at Gretchen. She felt like sticking her tongue out at him, but settled for an icy death glare. She turned on her heel and returned to the sales office. Customers were becoming more infrequent as the fall turned into winter. The tourists were long gone and most of their more recent sales had been to locals.

When Parker returned to the office, she glared at him behind his back and then went back to watching the parking lot for potential clients.

When the next car drove in, they raced out to the parking lot. She got there first and Parker skidded to a stop behind her. Before they could say anything, the couple in the car looked at the well-dressed people running at them like zombies were chasing them, got back into their car and drove away.

In their hurry to get to the potential customers, Gretchen hadn't heard another car enter the parking area.

"You've got to be kidding me," Charlotte said, with her eyebrows raised. "You guys are acting like children. I knew you weren't getting along, but this is ridiculous."

She winced. Charlotte was right. What were they doing?

"Hi, sis. Did we have plans for lunch?" Parker pointed at the two large plastic bags Charlotte was carrying.

"No, I brought you both Chinese takeout. I thought you could use a break. Come on." She motioned for them to follow her inside.

They nodded meekly and followed her to the kitchen of the demo home. She set white paper boxes of chicken fried rice, sweet and sour pork and chow mein noodles on the counter. While Charlotte grabbed plates out of the cupboard, Parker unpacked the last two boxes. Broccoli beef and almond chicken. Yum. Gretchen's mouth watered. She needed to eat. Dahlia would kill her if they had to resize her bridesmaid dress again.

They dished up their food and sat down at the kitchen table. The room was silent except for the sound of chewing.

When they were about halfway through with their meals, Charlotte spoke. "You can't keep doing this." She turned to Gretchen. "You're a mess working two jobs. You've looked sickly for months and I'm willing to bet it's all because of stress."

Gretchen nodded. She'd tried to hide how exhausted she was, but she could no longer cover the dark circles under her eyes with makeup.

"And you." Charlotte addressed her brother. "You've turned into someone I don't know. I saw you run to get to that customer before Gretchen. The old you would never have done that. You're acting like Graham."

He reddened.

Charlotte scooped the last bite of food into her mouth and placed her plate in the sink. "You need to figure this out. There's still work left to do here and you need a better working relationship because this isn't good for either of you." She flounced out of the model home.

After she left, Gretchen pushed the food around her plate with her fork. She glanced at Parker out of the corner of her eye. He continued to eat, chewing slower than she'd have thought possible. Was he prolonging the meal to avoid talking with her?

"Parker," she said. He looked up.

"Gretchen, I'm sorry." He sighed and pushed his plate away. "This isn't how I thought it would be. I figured we could work together, even if we weren't dating." He stood, pushed his chair in and paced the floor. "I don't want to fight anymore. You can have the remaining sales. I've been a jerk."

Although he was saying exactly what she'd dreamed of hearing, she knew he wasn't entirely at fault.

"I wasn't behaving well either. Let's split the remaining commissions and the sales incentive bonus. Deal?" She stuck out her hand.

He grinned and shook her hand. "Deal."

"I'm going to go to the closet in the back room and organize our remaining sales materials, okay?"

He nodded.

Once she was safely out of the room, tears poured from her eyes. She hated that Charlotte was right. They'd let their silly fight get completely out of hand and become unprofessional. They'd even lost a potential client today with their behavior. She counted the floor plan brochures and stacked them in neat piles. While they'd had about twenty boxes in the walk-in closet at the start of the summer, they were now down to one. The sales job was almost over and it was time she started thinking of the future. She had almost enough saved to move to Seattle. In fact, she could probably move in December, but Dahlia would kill her if she moved so close to the wedding. So, January it was. After the New Year, she'd start a new life in Seattle, away from her family and friends.

More tears streamed down her face. This was what she wanted, right? A chance for something different, a new beginning. But it felt like she'd already tried something new with the sales job and it had made her crazy. She dried her tears on the sleeve of her sweater. The exhaustion was getting to her. Things would work out and she'd find the right path.

20

A week later, Gretchen lined up bottles of Chardonnay, Merlot, Riesling and Shiraz on the counter in the model home. All were from a local winery. To sell the remaining three home sites, they'd organized a complimentary afternoon wine and cheese event for anyone who stopped by the development. They'd advertised the event in both the Candle Beach and Haven Shores newspapers and had high hopes for a good turnout.

The flow of potential customers had slowed to a trickle and the last three lots had proven difficult to sell. Some days, they didn't even have one visitor. This last push had to work, or it would be a long winter.

Parker placed a glass tray containing an assortment of cheeses, grapes and thinly sliced apple wedges on the counter. She scooted a plate of Brie and tray of crackers closer to the cheeses, then swiped a piece of sharp cheddar and a water cracker and crossed the kitchen to the window.

Outside, thunderclouds hung low in the sky, threatening to dump rain at any time. Angry winds stirred up white caps on the blue-gray ocean. It definitely wasn't summer anymore. Parker came up behind her.

"It looks like it's going to pour." She gazed outside again. "No one is going to come today if it's raining."

He placed his hands on her shoulders and peered at the sky. "It'll hold off for a while. We should get some people. Relax. You've lived here all your life, you know what November is like. Dreary weather won't keep people around here from showing up."

His touch and words reassured her. Ever since Charlotte had lectured them about how they'd been acting, she and Parker had almost become friends again. At times like this, she even remembered why they'd dated. But that was a long time ago. Soon, if this event worked to drum up business, she'd be moving to Seattle. What had previously seemed so far away now loomed directly in front of her.

Several hours passed by before they finally had a visitor. A man came in, brushing rain off his jacket. "I saw your sign on the road," he said. "I've been wanting to check out the progress up here, and now seemed like as good a time as any."

"Well, we're glad you were able to make it." She handed him a paper appetizer plate. It didn't sound like he was a serious home buyer, but at this point, she'd take anything.

"We have a few home sites left," Parker said. "Would you like to take a look at them?"

The man plopped a grape in his mouth and looked out the window. Fat raindrops fell from the sky. "I'd intended to, but maybe I'll just take a look at some floor plans today. The weather doesn't seem to be cooperating."

"Sure, no problem." Gretchen led him over to her desk and after asking him a few questions, found a floor plan that suited his needs.

"Thanks. I'll show it to my wife. We've been saving for years for a place on the water, and I think she'll really like this layout." He looked longingly at the cheese plate. "Do you mind?"

She laughed. "Go ahead. I don't think we'll have many takers today."

The man thanked her, grabbed a handful of cheese and crackers and left.

"The weather not cooperating is an understatement," Parker said. Outside, the sky had darkened and the plump raindrops had turned into a solid sheet of rain. A gust of wind roared past, shaking the house. They walked out onto the covered porch to view the storm.

In the forests down by the highway, the trees bent and swayed as the wind blasted them. The ocean waves had become a frenzied mass of whitecaps and she could barely see where each wave started and ended. They returned to the toasty warm living room.

"Maybe we should close it down for the day," Parker said. "It's getting dark and I doubt anyone else will come." They stared at the remaining food.

"So much for that idea," Gretchen said. "Now what?"

He shrugged. "I don't know. We'll figure something out. We can try again next week."

As soon as they had the food in the refrigerator, the power flickered and then went out.

"Good timing," she said.

"We'd better get home before things get worse."

On the street outside, the wind blew branches and leaves across the pavement. They dashed for their cars, but she hesitated outside of hers.

"I forgot to get something," she shouted to Parker. "Go ahead and leave."

He drove down the hill away from the houses and she ran back inside. In all the commotion, she'd left her laptop in the model home. She unplugged the laptop and shoved it into her messenger bag. Something moderately big, maybe a tree branch, bounced off the roof. She shuffled through the papers on her desk. She wanted to make sure she had everything she'd need if the storm was bad enough to keep them from work the next day.

Headlights appeared in the driveway. A minute later, Parker darted in with the hood of his raincoat pulled tightly over his head.

"We can't get out."

"What do you mean we can't get out?" She stopped packing. She moved closer to the door to see Parker more clearly.

"I mean there's no way to get out. There are at least two huge trees down over the entrance, right before the road meets the highway. We can't drive anywhere."

"Maybe we could call someone to pick us up by the gate."

"Maybe." He tapped his phone. "No service."

"No service?" she echoed. "So we're stuck here for the night?"

"Looks that way. But hey, at least we've got plenty of food and I think I've got some blankets in my car. There are worse places to be stuck."

She was stranded here all night with Parker? The wind howled outside and rain splattered the windows. For once, she was glad that the property had been practically clear cut. If two trees had fallen on the road, who knew how many more would fall by the time the storm was over. She pressed her face against the window and watched nature's fury.

"Pretty impressive," he said as he came up behind her. "I love these winter storms."

"Me too." When she was a child, she and her dad used to dress in full rain gear and go down to the beach overlook to watch the waves beat upon the shore. She turned away from the window and accidentally brushed against Parker's chest, causing an all too familiar surge throughout her body. She couldn't deny their strong chemistry, so she'd tried to avoid any chance of physical contact with him in their daily interactions. Had he noticed her reaction to his touch? It didn't appear that he had.

"I'll get the flashlights." Anything to keep him from seeing her flushed face.

He nodded. She used the light from her cellphone to light the way to the back bedroom. She knew there was a flashlight in their emergency supplies. If she could find it, that was.

This bedroom had been outfitted with a desk and rolling chair to resemble an office. The shades were down, casting the room into complete darkness with the exception of the glow from her phone's screen. She opened the closet door and searched for the emergency kit.

Aha. There it was. She stood on her tiptoes and pulled it down. It felt light and she had a sinking feeling that she wasn't going to find the flashlight in it. After unzipping the bag and confirming her suspicions, she tossed it back into the closet. Now what?

She made her way back to the living room.

"No flashlight?"

"It wasn't in the emergency supplies."

"I was afraid of that," he said. "Martin borrowed it one night to check something out on one of the houses and he must not have returned it."

"I might have something in my car." She looked out the

window at the rainstorm and frowned. The rain would soak her in a minute and she hated being wet.

He snapped his fingers. "I've got an idea." He dug in the kitchen drawer and pulled out a book of matches. Striking a match, he lit the wick on one of the decorative candles in the middle of the dining room table.

"You're destroying the aura of perfection," she teased.

"Hey, there aren't many houses left to sell, and I think this is a good enough reason to light a prop on fire." He smiled at her. The candle flickered, casting shadows on his face. Then he flicked the switch to turn on the gas fireplace. The blower didn't work, but it still produced a fair amount of heat and cast a cheery glow a few feet in front of it.

She scanned the room. "What do we do now?"

"We've got food, water, heat, and good company. What more could we want?" He gestured across the room. "I think I even saw some prop games in the family room. I'll check, okay?"

She nodded. "I hope they're real and not fake like the bed in the master bedroom."

She knew they were perfectly safe in the model home, but it felt strange to not have anyone know where they were. Her cell phone still wasn't getting reception. She moved the candle to an end table and sat down on the couch. Parker came into the room carrying two games and held them out to her.

"I've got Monopoly or Aggravation—what's your poison?"

She looked from one to the other. When she was a kid, her family had played some rousing games of Aggravation. She pointed to the game. "That one."

"Aggravation it is." He left Monopoly on the kitchen counter and set Aggravation in front of her on the coffee table. "I'm a little hungry. Do you want some cheese and crackers?"

"Yeah, that would be great, thanks."

He returned first with two glasses of Merlot and handed one to her.

"Thanks." She folded her legs up beneath her on the couch and relaxed into the puffy cushions. He was right. There were worse places to be marooned. He brought the food over to the table and she set up the game.

"Well, now I'm glad that we had so few people today." She stuffed a gorgonzola-topped cracker into her mouth and followed it with a sliver of apple.

"No kidding," he said as he mowed through a plate of cheese and crackers. He brushed crumbs away from his mouth and sipped his wine. "Now let's get on with the game. I'm going to cream you."

"We'll see about that," she countered. Her face was flushed from the heat of the gas fireplace and the alcohol had relaxed her. "I don't plan on going easy on you. In fact, let's make a bet on it. If I win, you have to sleep on the floor. I get the couch."

"Fair enough. And if I win, you have to go out on a date with me."

Awkward silence followed his proclamation. Finally, she said, "Parker, you know it won't work between us. We've already tried this."

"I know, but soon we won't have this job between us." He waved his hands in the air. "Gretchen, I've tried to forget about you, but I can't."

She smiled shakily at him. "Fine, I'll go out with you if you win. But I don't plan on letting you win."

"I'm counting on it, but I must tell you, I'm really good at this game." He grinned and rolled the dice.

He hadn't been kidding. Time after time, his playing piece landed on hers, sending her back to Start.

"Give me a break here." She laughed and rolled again. She was losing badly. Slowly, she regained ground until they were tied. On her turn, she rolled a three, sending her last piece home. "Comfy couch, here I come."

"I guess it's the floor for me." He looked disappointed.

She glanced out the window. "Hey, I think the rain's stopped. Do you want to get a closer look at the surf? I bet the view is breathtaking from the houses down in the Cliffside area."

"Sure," he agreed and gave her a lopsided grin that made her heart catch. "Let's go." He reached out for her hand and pulled her to standing, holding her fingers a little longer than necessary. A warmth spread through her bones that had nothing to do with the heat from the fireplace.

They ventured outside into the wind. The rain had finally stopped, but angry thunderclouds over the ocean promised another round. Leaves and tree branches littered the streets like a tornado had passed through. Other than the wind and waves, it was eerily quiet. The clouds had parted above them, leaving the sky temporarily clear. Moonlight lit their path as they walked down the hill to the new Cliffside homes. One of the houses was still under construction and they climbed up onto the uncovered back deck and perched on an open window frame to watch the storm.

"I can't believe people are going to be moving in soon." Gretchen twisted her neck to view the other houses. "It's amazing how fast everything goes."

"I know. Time does fly by all too fast." Parker shifted his

body to face her. "I know you thought I was joking about the date, but I'd really like us to try again. I care about you." He touched her shoulder to get her to look at him. "Tell me you don't have feelings for me too?"

She stared at him, not sure how to respond. It had been months since she'd found out he'd lied about the job. Could she look past him not telling her the truth? When her ex-boyfriend had cheated on her and lied about it for months, she'd been devastated. But was what Parker had done as bad as that?

"Look, I know you're still upset about my mother telling me about the interview. But you have to believe me—I already had an interview scheduled, long before I met you."

She searched his face. Was he telling the truth? She saw nothing but regret and hope in his eyes—not a trace of dishonesty. With the exception of the interview situation, she'd never known him to be anything less than truthful. "What do you mean that you already had an interview scheduled?" She watched him carefully.

"I met Martin the week before we met. That's why I was in Candle Beach for the chocolate festival. I wanted to get a feel for the local community before my interview." He looked her straight in the eye.

"You're serious," she said slowly. Her heart beat faster. "Why didn't you tell me this before?"

"I tried. You didn't want to hear it." He sighed. "I can't control what my mother does, but know this—I truly thought it would be better for you not to know about her interference."

She trembled. Had she been wrong about him all this time? Should she forgive him? She peered out at the ocean, hoping for an answer. The ocean churned with the wind's fury. The moonlight cast a creamy glow on the inky waves, rivaling any winter storm she'd seen in the past. It amazed her how the seasons could change the ocean so drastically, from often placid seas in the summer to this—powerful surges that could move a giant tree with a single push from the tide.

One little misunderstanding had torn them apart. Could they come together just as quickly? Was she ready to forgive him?

He put his hand on her leg, bringing back her attention. "Gretchen?" He stroked her hair away from her face and she leaned into his hand. She couldn't resist him any longer.

"I'm sorry I was so rough on you." Her lips parted and she gazed at him under heavy eyelids.

"Me too. I definitely could have handled things better, but I'd really like to get past that." He tilted her chin and kissed her.

His lips felt soft and firm against hers. She caressed his cheek. The five o'clock shadow scratched her palm, amplifying her already alert senses. The wind blew across the porch, tangling her dark hair against him. He brushed her hair back and pulled her closer. She tuned out the roaring of the waves and wind. Nothing mattered but him.

"I've been waiting so long to do this." He cupped her face and deepened the kiss. She wrapped her arms around his neck and allowed herself to succumb to his lips, captured by a force so strong that she feared she might drown in the waves of desire. She'd had romantic relationships before, but nothing had prepared her for this. If only she'd listened to his explanation before. They'd lost so much time that they could have spent together.

Icy raindrops pelted them, but the only thing she felt was the heat from his body. When their clothing was completely drenched and her hair hung down in sodden strands, he broke the embrace.

"We should probably find someplace a little drier," he said.

She stared at him. What had he said? Through hazed eyes, she glanced down at her clothing, noticing the water accumulating in the fabric for the first time.

He wiped a drop of rain off of her lip and she playfully kissed his thumb.

"We can continue this back at the sales office," he promised. He grabbed her hand and led her back to the street. Giggling like little kids, they ran hand in hand back to the model home. She ran slightly ahead of him, giving him a chance to see her fully in the dim light. The thin cotton blouse and dress pants she was wearing had molded to her body, revealing a curvy figure that he wanted to see more of. She paused and lifted her face to the sky, opening her mouth to taste the rain. He couldn't remember the last time he'd seen such unadulterated joy on a woman's face. How had he gotten so lucky to find her?

She turned to him and laughed. "I haven't been this soaked in a long time." He pulled lightly on her hand and spun her around until their torsos were pressed together. Rain streamed down their faces as their lips met again, concealing the tears of happiness that had welled in the corners of his eyes. Even in the miserable storm conditions, he didn't want to waste a second with her.

They reached the covered front porch of the model home. Underneath the protection of the roof, she pulled the tail of her blouse out of her pants and attempted to wring the water out, revealing a small patch of pale skin above her waistline. His pulse quickened.

"It's useless," she said, dropping the twisted, waterlogged fabric against her body. "We're never going to dry if we leave these wet clothes on."

"I have a suggestion for that." He winked at her.

She tapped him on the arm and laughed. "There are some towels in the bathroom. Thank goodness they're real and not cardboard. We can wear them while our clothes dry."

"Not exactly what I had in mind, but I guess that could work too."

Her face was flushed from running up the hill from the Cliffside lots. The rain had washed away any trace of makeup on her skin, leaving only her own natural beauty. He couldn't stop himself from touching her again. He swung her off her feet and kissed her until she was breathless. When he set her back down, it took her a moment to regain her footing.

"Need some help?" he asked.

She stepped back and shook her finger at him. "Uh-uh. Help like yours I can do without. I've got to get out of these clothes before I catch pneumonia." She pushed open the door, smiled slyly at him and scampered into the house.

He stood on the porch for a few minutes to regain his composure before following her inside. He'd never thought he'd find a woman like her and then as soon as he had, he'd lost her. Now, she was his, all his, and he wasn't going to ever let her go again.

21

A week later

"Hi girls," Gretchen sang out as she breezed into Off the Vine. Maggie and Dahlia were already seated at their usual table. They exchanged knowing glances that she pretended not to see.

"Charlotte called and said she's running a little late," Maggie said.

"Not surprising." Gretchen slid into the booth next to Dahlia.

"Hey, are you guys talking smack about me?" Charlotte said, coming up behind them.

"You're not known for your timeliness." Maggie patted the seat next to her. "Sit."

"Hey, I was only a couple minutes late. And I called."

"We're just messing with you," Dahlia said. "We're glad you were able to make it. Especially since we were just about to have Gretchen tell us about her date with Parker last night."

"A lady never kisses and tells," Gretchen said primly.

"Right..." Dahlia laughed.

"I for one am glad not to hear the details. That's my brother you're talking about." Charlotte made a disgusted face and then giggled.

"Alright girls, let's leave her alone," Maggie said. "I'm starving. What are we going to order?"

They flagged down the waitress and placed their order.

"I do have some news though." Gretchen looked around the table, building suspense.

"Oh my gosh, you're getting married!" Dahlia cried out.

"No." She shot her friend an exasperated look. "We've only been together for a week. Maybe we'll get married someday, but not any time soon."

Maggie said under her breath, "A week-long relationship that was eight months in the making."

Gretchen glared at her, but couldn't hide her smile.

"So what's the news?" Charlotte asked.

"Parker and I are starting a new real estate company. We figured we navigated all the kinks in our professional relationship over the last eight months, so we know what we're getting into. We'll be focused on selling real estate in Haven Shores and Candle Beach. We were worried about how our parents would react, but both sets want us to stay in the area and are excited about us entering the local market."

Dahlia squealed. "You're staying in Candle Beach?"

"Yes." She beamed. It was the right decision. She had no doubts now about Parker or staying in her hometown. It wasn't that she had necessarily wanted to be in Seattle, it was more of a need for something in her life to change. Now that she had Parker and a new business, life was good.

"Well," Charlotte said. "Let's celebrate."

They clinked their glasses together. "To happiness in Candle Beach."

The next morning, Gretchen drove down to Haven Shores to have brunch with Parker. They met at Arturo's, where they'd gone on their first official date. After eating, they walked out to the boardwalk, hand in hand. The winter sun shone down on the beach, making the minuscule particles of mica in the sand glow like someone had tossed glitter over the railing. A few people walked along the hard-packed sand at the shoreline. Everything looked so different in the daylight.

"Still glad you gave me another chance?" Parker peered into her eyes.

She threw her arms around his neck. "Yes. You've made me happier than I could ever imagine."

"I feel the same way." He kissed her sweetly on the lips and she snuggled in closer.

"Now if we can just get our parents to stop their feud." She sighed. That would be a long shot.

He cocked his head to the side. "You didn't know?"

"What?"

"Your mom called my parents and arranged for them to have dinner at their house in Candle Beach next Friday."

She shook her head. "That ought to be interesting."

"Hey, they're trying. We've managed to make it work. They can too." He kissed her again. "They've taken the first steps—that's what counts."

Tears of happiness pooled in the corners of her eyes. How had everything come together? They'd gone through so much, from their first magical date to all of the misunderstandings, and then come back again full circle.

"Hey, Parker," she said.

"What?" He stepped back to gaze into her eyes, still holding her hand.

"I love you."

"I love you too." He guided her over to the railing and wrapped his arms around her, their hands meeting in front of her on the weather-beaten wood. He kissed the top of her head and she leaned back against his chest, his embrace making her feel safe and warm.

They watched the waves crash against the shore, no two alike. She knew things wouldn't always be perfect between them or with anything else in life, but whatever the future brought them, they'd make it through together.

**THANK YOU FOR READING SWEET
SUCCESS!**

Want to spend more time in Candle Beach?

Dahlia's Story: Sweet Beginnings

Maggie's Story: Sweet Promises
    See the next page for a preview of Sweet Promises

Available on Amazon and Kindle Unlimited

SWEET PROMISES: A CANDLE BEACH SWEET ROMANCE

"*A*lbert, I need those turkeys by Wednesday." Maggie Price leaned back in the chair with the phone pressed to her ear and tapped a pen against the wooden desk. The phone beeped insistently to alert her to another call. Whoever it was would have to wait. This call with her supplier was too important to interrupt.

"Look, I'm sorry, but there's nothing I can do about it." The man on the other end of the phone call sighed. "You're not going to have them by Thanksgiving. I might be able to get you something else, but with that storm dumping snow in Portland, there's no way that we'll be able to get the turkeys to you in time. Nothing's getting through."

"I'll see if I can get someone else to deliver them," she said. "I'll talk to you tomorrow, okay?"

"Maggie, you know I'd get them for you if I could, but my hands are tied. I'm sorry." He sighed again.

"I know. Thanks for trying." She hung up the phone and stared at the ceiling in her tiny office. Although no cobwebs hung from the corners, the paint had worn thin in places and the office showed its age. When she'd bought the Greasy Spoon from the former owner and revamped it into the Bluebonnet Café, she'd put all her money and efforts into the customer-facing portions of the café and kitchen, leaving no spare cash for anything behind the scenes. She shook her head. There were bigger problems at the moment than scratched paint.

What was she going to do with no turkeys to serve for Thanksgiving dinner at the café? There'd be a rebellion in Candle Beach. Many of the townspeople didn't have relatives close by and they counted on having their holiday dinner at her restaurant. She stared blankly at the computer screen, which showed her order for the turkeys that wouldn't be arriving any time soon.

Someone knocked on the door. She regarded it wearily. What now?

"Come in."

"Maggie?" Her lead waitress, Belinda, pushed the door open, sending the aroma of freshly baked apple pies throughout the office. Maggie's stomach grumbled. Lunch had been hours ago. She pasted an 'everything's alright' smile on her face for her employee's benefit.

"What's going on?"

"It's your mom. She said she can't watch Alex any longer today—she's got to get to work." Belinda looked apologetic. "She said you were supposed to be there an hour ago."

Maggie shot a glance at the old-fashioned analog clock on the wall and jumped out of her chair. Dealing with the supply snafu had taken longer than she'd thought.

"It's six thirty already? Is she still on the phone?"

"Yeah, I put her on hold," Belinda said. "You've been in here since I started my dinner shift at five. Is everything okay?"

"Things are fine. Can you please tell her I'll be there in less than ten minutes?" She threw on her winter jacket and rushed past Belinda. "Thanks!"

"Sure, I'll let her know," Belinda called after her.

Everything was not okay. A winter storm south of them in Oregon had ground all of her suppliers' trucks to a halt. She'd been trying to improvise on their daily menu, but something had to give. She'd even had to send someone to the local grocery store to scrounge for hamburger buns that morning. The way it was going, they'd be having Spam and frozen peas for Thanksgiving dinner in two days. That would not go over well with her regulars.

The big holiday meals were always a pain to coordinate, but people in town who didn't have family or friends nearby appreciated her having the café open for them to eat at. She knew most of the people in this small town, either through the café or from growing up there, and she didn't want to let anyone down.

She drove the mile to her parents' house, her mind spinning with everything she needed to take care of. Juggling the schedule for the café and care for her six-year-old son, Alex, was a constant struggle. In a few weeks, he'd be off school for winter break and things would become even more complicated. She wasn't looking forward to that. As soon as she reached her parents' house, she parked crookedly in an empty parking spot and ran inside.

～

"Thank goodness you're here," Charlene Johansen,

Maggie's mom, said. "I've got to get to work at the market. I was supposed to be there thirty minutes ago."

"I'm sorry, Mom. I totally lost track of time. Things have been crazy at the café." Maggie felt horrible about being late. Having her mom babysit Alex was a lifesaver and she couldn't get along without her.

"It's okay, honey. One of my co-workers is covering for me, but I need to get there soon. Dad had to work late, or I'd have him take Alex." She searched her daughter's face. "What's going on?"

"Nothing, everything is fine."

"Really? Because you don't look so good."

Maggie opened her mouth to reply, but Alex came barreling around the corner. "Mommy! You have to see the new Lego set Grandma bought me. It's Minecraft!"

"Mom...you bought him more Legos?" She narrowed her eyes at her mother.

Charlene blushed. "He had the first of the two sets, so I bought him the second. He's my only grandchild. Let me spoil him a little." She kissed the top of Alex's head and patted her daughter's hand. "I've got to go. Lock up when you leave."

"Bye. Have fun at work." Maggie called to her. Then she turned to Alex. "C'mon kiddo. Let's get home and you can show me your new Legos while I make dinner." He ran off to the family room to get his toys and she leaned against the open door to wait for him.

"Got 'em." He pushed past her and she locked the door behind them. He ran ahead of her out to the driveway, opened the car door and got into his booster seat. Maggie sat in the driver's seat and stared at her son in the rearview mirror. Her husband Brian would have been amazed to see how much Alex had grown over the last five years. Brian had been an Army soldier. He died in the Middle East when Alex was a baby and never had the chance to see what a wonderful little person his son had become.

She put the car in reverse and drove home to the tiny two-bedroom apartment she shared with Alex. Candle Beach didn't have much in the way of large apartment complexes like in the big city, but she'd been lucky to find a place in a four-plex less than a mile from the café.

After admiring Alex's new Lego set, feeding him and getting him to bed, she was bushed. She grabbed her planning notebook and flopped on the couch, covering her legs with a lightweight afghan. She flipped on the TV while she worked on an updated menu for the café's Thanksgiving dinner. The TV provided background noise but she barely heard it.

The unsettled feeling she'd had all day kept nagging at her. She'd made the Bluebonnet Café a success, but she wanted something more. She'd volunteered to cater her friend Dahlia's wedding to test out a new catering business, hoping that it would fulfill her Type A personality's desire for a new challenge. And challenging it had been.

Running the café, starting a new catering business and being a single mother wasn't easy. Would she be able to do it all? She dropped her head to the pillowy couch arm and closed her eyes. Things would work out. She'd always found a way to get everything done in the past.

∿

The next morning, Maggie dropped Alex off at school and headed for the café. Only one day remained before Thanksgiving and she still didn't have a main course for the big holiday meal. She called every supplier in her notebook, but understandably, they were either sold out of turkeys at such late notice, or they had the same problem with the snow as her original supplier. Finally, after a few hours, she procured some hams that a supplier assured her would get there by the next day. They weren't what her customers would expect for Thanksgiving, but they'd have to do.

With that crisis averted, she finished planning the rest of the menu. Thank goodness they had potatoes. If there were no mashed potatoes as well as no turkey, there would be a riot for sure.

Her best pastry chef and right-hand woman, Bernadette, stuck her head past the half-opened door.

"Maggie? Do you have time?"

"Time for what?" Maggie set down her notebook. "If there's something wrong with the latest food shipment, I don't want to hear about it." She smiled to let her employee know she was kidding.

"No, no. Nothing like that." Bernadette grinned and approached her desk. "I'm scheduled to work on Friday, but my boyfriend invited me to go away for the weekend. Lily said she'd take my shift in the kitchen. Is that okay with you?"

Phew. Nothing major. She didn't think she could take anything else.

"Of course, go ahead. I hope you have fun." Lily wasn't as hard of a worker as Bernadette, but business should be slow on the Friday after Thanksgiving.

"Thanks!" Bernadette turned and sailed out of the room.

Maggie thought about starting in on the schedule for the week after next, but a quick glance at her watch changed her mind. Alex had a half day at school and she needed to pick him up soon.

"I'll be back after five," she called to her kitchen staff. They waved to show they'd heard, but continued working on orders from the lunch rush.

~

After she got Alex home, he ran off to his room to play and she collapsed on the couch. Her split shift days were exhausting. She always intended to rest on the couch while at home, but household chores or other projects tended to grab her attention. Today was no different. She'd stacked her supplies for Dahlia's bridal shower decorations and party favors in the corner, and the half-finished boxes for the petit fours mocked her.

She sighed. At least if she got them done today, there would be less to do on Friday night. She flipped on the TV and mindlessly watched an old Friends episode while folding the small boxes. She'd ordered the boxes and lids from a craft supply store in Haven Shores, but it hadn't occurred to her how much time it would take to assemble them. Gretchen had volunteered to help with the party favors, but she'd told her not to worry. In hindsight, she probably should have accepted the help.

Making the petit fours should be fun though. Before she'd had Alex, she'd been a bored Army wife, living in a community far away from all of her friends and family, with the exception of Brian. At their last duty station, she'd taken pastry-making and cake-decorating classes at the local culinary school. Now, other than the desserts she helped make for the café, she didn't have much call to make fancy cakes. She'd searched YouTube and found a 'how to' video for making petit fours. She planned to place four in each of the paper boxes. Then she'd wrap a ribbon around the outside and tie it neatly with a bow. She brightened. The final product would be worth it and the guests would love them.

By the time she needed to take Alex to her parents' house for the evening, she had finished forming the boxes, but there was still a long list of things to do for the shower. Tomorrow was Thanksgiving, and after she worked a morning shift, she and Alex would go to her parents' house for dinner. That left Friday. She eyed the pile of decorations. Yeah, plenty of time. She brushed off her hands and called down the hallway.

"Alex! Time to go."

"Do I have to?" Alex whined.

"Yes. Sorry buddy, but you're only six. I can't leave you home alone and I have to work."

"But Dylan's mom stays home with him. He gets to stay at home and play all day after school and not go anywhere else."

Maggie mentally counted to ten. "Well, I have to work. Now get your shoes on."

He grumbled more at her, but reluctantly put his shoes on. At times like this, Maggie really wished she had a partner to help parent Alex. Being the sole provider and caregiver for her little family was stressful, and someone else to share things with would make life much easier. Her parents were a big help, but it wasn't the same as having her husband home to help. She hadn't dated anyone since Brian and she wasn't sure if she wanted to, so gaining a partner was a far-off dream.

If business continued to do well at the café, she might be able to afford a house cleaner or a full-time nanny soon. That would help, but it wouldn't be the same as having someone to share everything with. *If wishes were horses*, she thought. She wasn't sure what it meant, but her mother said it often and it seemed appropriate for her current situation.

"I'm ready." Alex yanked the door open and sprinted out to the car, waiting impatiently for her to unlock the car door.

She beeped it from the front porch. At five o'clock, the sky had already darkened. The short days of winter were rough and she wished for some summer sun to brighten her day. At least winter meant the holidays, and after Thanksgiving was over, she was free to put up the Christmas tree and decorate with lights. Christmas was her favorite time of year. There was something enchanting about seeing lights adorning buildings and hearing Santa Claus ringing the bell for the Salvation Army outside the grocery store. Sometimes, it even snowed in Candle Beach, although being on the ocean, they didn't usually get much accumulation.

This year would be extra special, with Dahlia's wedding a week before Christmas. Not only was she catering the wedding, but she and another friend, Gretchen, were Dahlia's only bridesmaids. She pulled her coat closed and hurried to the car. There was so much to do—all the bridal shower and catering prep for Dahlia's wedding, the holiday decorating, and she still needed to buy a few stocking stuffers for Alex. She took a deep breath to calm herself and opened the car door, ready to receive another tongue lashing from her sixteen-year-old in a six-year-old's body.

~

Chapter Two

Jake Price knocked most of the snow off of his winter
boots, then removed them and set them outside the door
of his parents' house. Portland, Oregon had been hit
unusually hard by a recent snowstorm and the historic
Craftsman homes on the block looked like a Norman
Rockwell winter scene. He didn't bother to knock before
entering.

The telltale scent of a turkey roasting in the oven tanta-
lized his senses as soon as he pushed the door open. His
mother's voice led him to the kitchen, where she perched on
a bar stool with her back to him, talking to someone on
the phone.

"We'll still see you for Christmas, right?" Barbara Price
slumped slightly at whatever the caller said. "Only for two
days? Can Alex stay longer?"

Jake could hear the disappointment in her voice.

"Okay, honey, we'll talk to you later." She set the phone
on the counter and slid off the stool, resting against the bar.

"Mom," he said.

She put her hand to her chest and spun around to
face him.

"Don't sneak up on me like that. I'm an old woman."

"Not so old," he said, coming up to her and wrapping his
arms around her shoulders. She returned the hug and scru-
tinized him.

"Did you come by to do laundry? Thanksgiving dinner

doesn't start until one o'clock." She glanced at the clock. "It's only ten."

"No," he laughed. "I came by to give you a hand." He grabbed a red-and-green apron from a hook on the wall. "What can I do? Put me to work."

She beamed. "You can peel and quarter the potatoes. Your father usually does it, but I sent him to the store for butter." She shook her head. "I forgot to add it to the grocery list when he went to the market yesterday. Ah, I'm getting old." She rolled out a mound of dough sitting on the floured counter.

Jake tied the apron strings around his waist and sat down across from her at the bar. The potato peeler felt tiny in his large hands, but he quickly got the hang of it. He peeled a few potatoes and then asked, "Was that Maggie you were talking to? She's not coming to Thanksgiving this year? I'd hoped to see her. It's been a long time since we both came to a holiday meal."

His mother's smile slipped. "No, she's in charge of the restaurant today. She and Alex will come down to Portland for a few days at the end of December."

"But not for as much time as you'd like to see Alex, right?"

"Maggie's really busy. She'll bring him down here when she can. That girl has a lot on her plate." She hesitated. "She sounded more stressed than I've ever heard her. I wish I could go up there and help out with Alex, but I've got my job at the library. I think she may have bitten off more than she can chew this time. You know Maggie."

She busied herself preparing the lattice crust for an apple pie, but concern was etched across her face.

He did know Maggie, enough to know she was the most driven woman he'd ever met. When his younger brother

Brian brought her home at his college's Christmas break to meet the family the first time, she'd mapped out every minute of her time in Portland, determined to make the most of it. They'd affectionately called her 'Maggie the human dynamo' behind her back. Brian had been smitten from the moment he met her, and they got married in the December following his college graduation.

Jake had been stationed with the Army at Fort Lewis, Washington, at the time and had been able to get home for their wedding. Soon after they married, Brian had left for his Officer Basic Course in Missouri, taking Maggie with him.

A portrait of his brother in uniform sat on the mantel, drawing his attention. He and his parents had been devastated when Brian was killed in the Middle East and he couldn't imagine how Maggie had felt, especially with a little baby.

Before Brian deployed for the Middle East, his parents had hosted a family picnic in their backyard. He remembered it had been a bright, sunny summer day. A perfect kind of day, where nothing bad could happen. Maggie had worn a white sundress imprinted with red roses and carried Alex in a wrap around her front. He'd watched as Brian wrapped an arm around his wife and kissed his son on the forehead. His love for his family shone through in his actions and Jake had wondered if he himself would ever experience the same happiness.

After a neighbor drew Maggie into conversation, his brother had taken him aside and made him promise to take care of Maggie and Alex if something should happen to him. Jake had slugged him on the shoulder.

"You'll be fine, little bro. Nothing's going to happen to you." Jake had been on two tours to the Middle East himself and knew things weren't great over there, but he didn't want his brother to worry about leaving his wife and child behind.

"I know, but just the same, promise me you'll do this for me?" Brian had smiled, but his lips quivered as he patted Jake on the back. It was the last time they saw each other before Brian headed overseas.

When Brian didn't make it back, Jake intended to make good on his promise, but the Army had other ideas and stationed him in Korea for three years and then Germany for two. He'd kept up with Maggie and Alex's life through phone calls with his mother and he sent birthday cards to Alex, but his involvement hadn't extended past that. The years passed faster than he'd realized. After twenty years in the Army, he'd recently opted for retirement. Now here he was, back in the States, retired at the ripe old age of thirty-eight.

He gazed out the window at the empty snow-covered lawn, so different than his memory of the warm summer backyard picnic so many years ago. He returned his attention to his mother.

"I could go help with Alex for a few weeks."

"You?" She scoffed. "What do you know about kids?"

He shrugged. "I'll manage. I've been around kids before, you know."

Her demeanor softened. "What about your Border Patrol interview?"

"I'll head up there after my interview on Monday. I'm sure they won't call me back for a while. The federal government moves at the speed of a snail with their hiring process. I'd like to see Alex, and Maggie too, of course. It's been years since I saw him." He thought for a moment and counted the years. His brother had already been gone for five years? Alex would be about six now.

"Well, I'm sure Alex will be happy to see you. From what Maggie says, he'd love to have a man around. He's been wanting to play catch with someone and begging her to enroll him in Little League. Can you imagine Maggie playing softball?"

He could actually. He had a feeling his sister-in-law could do anything she set her mind to. But how would he do with a six-year-old? He'd spent time with the kids of an ex-girlfriend when they'd been dating, but it wasn't the same as with family. And that had been years ago. His ex hadn't been able to handle a long-distance relationship and they'd amicably broken up soon after he moved to Korea. He'd heard from friends that she was now happily married to a local guy.

"I have a few things to wrap up here, but I'll leave on Tuesday for Candle Beach. Don't say anything to Maggie though, okay? I want to surprise her and Alex."

His mother looked relieved. "I'm sure she'd welcome your help."

He wasn't convinced of that, but he knew he had to offer. He owed his brother that much.

"I can't wait until I retire. Only three years to go. Then I can visit Alex whenever I want. And maybe in a few years I'll have more grandkids...hint, hint." She eyed him.

He sighed. "When I can find a woman to stick with me. I haven't had much luck so far."

She patted him on the arm. "You'll find someone. You're a good man. The right woman is out there for you."

"Maybe." He was pushing forty. If he hadn't found the right woman yet, what were the odds he'd find her anytime soon? He'd had his share of romantic relationships, but most of them had been short-lived. Some due to the natural fizzling out of things, but most because of Army commitments. But the Army wasn't part of his life anymore, so now it was all on him. That thought both exhilarated and terrified him.

Made in the USA
San Bernardino, CA
09 January 2018